Hand over Fist
The Aagrah cookbook

ISBN 0-9549363-0-2

Published and distributed by ENDpapers

Collage Corner, 2 Norman Court,
York, YO1 7HU
ENGLAND

First published August 2005

Printed by **Fratelli Spada**, Rome.

the wit to **E**nquire
the wit to **N**ote
the wit to **D**iscern
works for the witful

END

www.endpapers.co.uk

Hand over Fist

The Aagrah cookbook
by Mohammed Aslam

FOREWORD

Brian J Turner CBE

PHOTOGRAPHY - TEXT LAYOUT - DESIGN

Catherine Lucas

EDITOR

Florence Millett

FOREWORD

Although we come from very different culinary styles, Aslam and I, as with lots of chefs, have so much in common.

For one thing, whenever you are preparing food for the public, the higher the quality and freshness of the food, the greater the pressure. And when you feel under pressure, a sense of surety is needed rather than one of panic. Surety is one of Aagrah's great qualities. You can always be sure the food will be good, the service superb and everything handled with confidence.

We have both been working steadily in this industry for more than 20 years, and just as my restaurants in Windsor and in Mayfair have helped elevate British cuisine, so Aagrah has been a big part of raising the awareness of Asian food in Britain and putting Bradford on the map as a great eating destination.

Aslam and I are both Yorkshiremen from fairly humble beginnings. We owe a lot to our families and we have had great loyalty and guidance from our supporters, often keeping us going when things have been tougher than we would have liked. We are both fortunate to have been blessed with finding the best platform to express our talents.

And the entire Aagrah family has done an enormous amount, not only to support Aslam in becoming the great chef he is, but beyond that, Aagrah as a group has been a steady contributor to the community. In common with our own Brian Turner Foundation, the Aagrah family has worked tirelessly to support many charitable organisations, both in the UK and overseas. Moreover, they are great ambassadors for Bradford, for Yorkshire, and for the north of England as a whole.

It is a pleasure to contribute a foreword to this book, which stands for a career and a set of values that I empathise with. I am sure that in the recipes you will find some great ideas for cooking, and in the Aagrah story, real inspiration.

Brian Turner CBE
August 2005

INTRODUCTION

I arrived in this great country in the 1960s, from a very humble family that had experienced extreme poverty throughout many generations. I had tears in my eyes and an obscure horizon ahead of me, but I put aside my emotions and misgivings and moved forward. Despite there being few resources available to me, all I felt within me was the will to achieve and to succeed.

I started working in the textile mills and later became a bus driver. In 1976, I finally started a mobile takeaway called Spice Pot in Bradford. Though it was my own business, I was not content. The cold weather and constant insults got the better of me. I wanted to achieve something bigger. I had the blessings of my poor family, the support of my wife and the inner desire to persist and to move forward.

In 1977, I opened the Aagrah in Shipley as a joint venture. Although the partnership grew through trust and commitment, unfortunately we did little business, and in 1981 the partnership ended and I took over the restaurant. The sole advice to buy the business came from my only son, Sajid. Sajid was a disabled child, but his insistence that I buy out my partner will remain the defining moment in the history of Aagrah. My wife became my rock as I began to build up what was essentially a broken business. It was tough to balance all of our commitments to Aagrah and to my son, but somehow we managed.

At the end of 1982, Drew Smith, the author of the Good Food Guide, backed by the Consumer Association, visited Bradford and gave a damning report on the food industry in the city. I felt it was an unjust and biased report. With the help of some leading Yorkshire dignitaries and the local council, I challenged Drew Smith to revisit Bradford and examine the wider picture concerning the food industry. He returned within the year and Aagrah was awarded 11 points out of 20, the best performing Asian restaurant in his consumer guide-book. Together with the local media and city council, we managed to wipe away the scar that had been left by his previous report. This gave me the drive and ambition to go further. A once blurred horizon was getting clearer, and my goal of becoming the best at what I did was ever closer. A formerly dejected member of the family was now becoming a successful businessman.

The business was growing and needed support. My brother, Aslam, who was working in the buses at the time, had previously worked at Aagrah in Shipley. I needed a partner, and in 1983 I asked Aslam to join me. I admired his commitment, hard work and honesty. Under my supervision, Aslam quickly learned the restaurant trade. This was further supported by another family member, Zafar Iqbal. Aslam brought vigour, enthusiasm and light into our growing business. His dedication and tremendous capacity for teamwork have proved invaluable. Aslam, Zafar, Arshad and more than 12 members of my family have all worked together as partners, and today we have a thriving business of 10 restaurants throughout the north of England.

Mohammed Sabir
Group Chairman

5

- For extra information on how to make these recipes, see Aslam's Cooking Tips and Advice, pages 8-9 and Editor's Cheat Notes, pages 92-93.
- All recipes in this book are based on 4 people eating. To accommodate greater or fewer numbers of diners, simply increase or decrease the ingredients accordingly.
- Dst sp is used throughout the recipes as an abbreviation for dessertspoon.
- Substitutions can be made within any recipe to accommodate individual preferences or restrictive diets. Specific suggestions have been made throughout the text (marked **optional** in the contents), but cooks should feel free to experiment with any recipe.
- If you have dietary restrictions, please continue to check the labels of any products you use whilst making recipes from this cookbook.

ASLAM'S COOKING TIPS AND ADVICE

Measurements

Instead of using more traditional measuring methods, such as scales, I decided to use a dessertspoon as the standard measuring unit throughout these recipes. I wanted to simplify the cooking process for those who wished to try and make South Asian food at home. As we all know, most household kitchens do not have scales, and so, if scales were needed, many people would not be able to attempt this small challenge of cooking at home. Moreover, cooking at home doesn't require such accuracy and precision as the bulk cooking and packing necessary for restaurants and supermarkets. One of the purposes of this book is to make the kitchen fun so that people enjoy cooking and don't feel like they're working in a laboratory!

It is also necessary to be confident. Trusting instinct over precision in the kitchen is a challenge, but, with practice, it is a much more efficient and rewarding way of cooking.

Tips on herbs and spices

- Always buy whole spices.
- Grind whole spices as and when you need them – the shelf life of whole spices is much longer than ground.
- Store spices in airtight containers at room temperature. If stored well, the shelf life of whole spices is around 2 years, compared with ground spices, which only retain their potency for 3-6 months.
- If a recipe demands that spices be roasted, place them in a dry pan on a very low heat for just a few minutes, until they become light brown. Do not over-roast, as the spices will become very bitter and lose their flavour.
- In some dishes whole spices are used, which is another advantage of buying your spices whole.
- Note that excessive use of herbs and spices can damage the taste of a dish. Take care not to exceed the appropriate/recommended quantities.

Purchase of vegetables and meat

As an experienced chef, I recommend that you always buy and use fresh vegetables, not frozen. The same goes for meat. The most obvious reason for this is the huge difference in taste between fresh and frozen foods. Fresh are infinitely tastier. Additionally, there have recently been questions over the provenance of frozen meat. It has been found that some chicken fillets arriving from mainland Europe have been injected with pork, which is neither halal nor kosher, as well as being fundamentally dishonest.

Preparation

Like any task, important or menial, preparation beforehand is as vital as doing the job itself. It is worth spending some time on preparation when cooking, and making sure that everything you need is easily accessible. This will make the whole process smoother and the recipes easy to follow. Here are a few tips to help you prepare:

- Gather all the herbs and spices required for the recipe or recipes.
- Slice or chop the vegetables and herbs beforehand and keep to one side.
- Try to separate the ingredients into groups according to the order in which they appear in the method.
- To avoid burning the spices, always keep a jug of water handy.

Some facts about health and nutrition of South Asian food

There is a common misconception that South Asian food is unhealthy. If it were, the whole of the Asian subcontinent would be full of obese people, and it is not.

One of the main reasons for this misapprehension is that the food in Asian restaurants is usually comparatively inexpensive (as well as delicious!), so it is easy and tempting to order copious amounts.

However, an often overlooked element of any foreign cuisine is the eating tradition associated with that cuisine. Without being educated in the traditions of Asian food, people can easily be unaware that, contrary to the accepted practice in the UK, in Asia, breads and rice comprise the main part of the meal and curries are intended solely as flavours to accompany these. The balance between breads and/or rice and curries is paramount. This divergence in customs has probably helped contribute to the false impression that curry is unhealthy. As with all foods, from whatever cuisine, care must always be taken not to consume in excess.

Finally, chefs can make food unhealthy by adding more than the required quantity of oil, ghee, salt, and so on. As a chef and restaurateur, I believe that obesity is due to lifestyle, overeating and lack of awareness of dietary customs and traditions. At Aagrah, we take seriously our responsibility to present not only delicious food, but also food that is wholesome, healthy and contributes to our customers' overall wellbeing.

Mohammed Aslam
Aagrah Director

Past

There have been a number of qualities that have allowed us, an immigrant family, to grow in our host country, such that we now consider ourselves Bradfordians. For if we are from anywhere, we are from West Yorkshire.

The first of these qualities is a sense of past, or history.

Sabir has included in his introduction several of the turning points in the development of Aagrah. 1972 was one, when we decided to leave the textile industry and join Bradford Transport. Apart from improved working conditions compared with the textile mills, the extraordinary good fortune this change brought us was working in public service and the company of other bus drivers. Of the Asian staff employed, the vast majority were university graduates from India and Pakistan. At break times, the employees largely broke into two groups – those with newspapers and lively informed discussion, and those playing cards and gambling their wages. I have to say I learned an immense amount from participating in both.

I also learned a great deal from having to speak to the public.

Another decisive moment was when I left Bradford to work with London Transport, while Sabir continued to run the restaurant in Shipley. From London I advised Sabir to sell the restaurant. I told him it was "rubbish", or words to that effect! A third turning point was when I finally went to help him in Shipley and something clicked. I began to do the food prep for the chef and to watch him as he worked. This was the beginning of my passion for food.

Remembering who you are and where you come from is a key quality in success. By that I don't mean that our family came from Kashmir, although of course that is true. What I mean is that we came from very little in terms of opportunity and resources. I think it is this that informs our commitment to the Aagrah organisation being a family in the widest sense, which includes staff and customers, and also to our fund-raising and our dedication to developing educational opportunities.

Finally, in Aagrah's past there has been a particular person who inspired us all. None of us will ever forget my nephew, Sabir's son, Sajid Mahmood, who was physically handicapped and died in 1983 and whose picture is on the cover of this book. His memory has prompted us to host events over the last 18 years that have raised over £250,000 for good causes. Had my nephew not challenged my brother when he sold our first restaurant to his business partner by shouting "YOU'VE SOLD MY RESTAURANT! YOU'VE SOLD MY RESTAURANT!", Sabir would not have bought it back, and our lives today would be very different and our family not as united.

Sajid's memory also continues to remind us that even the so-called 'least' among us may exert the greatest influence if we only listen.

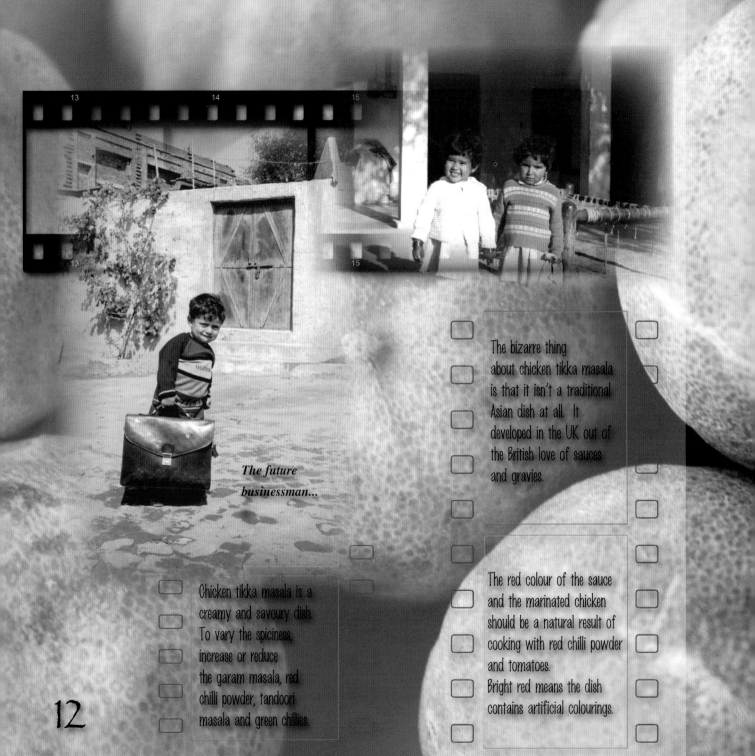

The future businessman...

The bizarre thing about chicken tikka masala is that it isn't a traditional Asian dish at all. It developed in the UK out of the British love of sauces and gravies.

Chicken tikka masala is a creamy and savoury dish. To vary the spiciness, increase or reduce the garam masala, red chilli powder, tandoori masala and green chillies.

The red colour of the sauce and the marinated chicken should be a natural result of cooking with red chilli powder and tomatoes. Bright red means the dish contains artificial colourings.

CHICKEN TIKKA MASALA

Ingredients

1kg	Chicken breast, diced
4	Dst sp vegetable oil
3	Large onions, finely chopped
½	Dst sp garlic puree (see recipe)
½	Dst sp ginger puree (see recipe)
2	Tomatoes, chopped
½	Dst sp coriander seeds, ground
¼	Dst sp cumin seeds, ground
¼	Dst sp garam masala
¼	Dst sp red chilli powder
½	Dst sp tandoori masala
½	Dst sp turmeric powder
2	Fresh green chillies, chopped
1	Handful of fresh coriander, chopped
½	Dst sp dried fenugreek leaves
½	Dst sp almonds, ground
½	Dst sp pistachio nuts, ground
4	Dst sp single cream
¼	Dst sp salt

Ingredients for marinade

1	Dst sp mustard oil
1	Dst sp garlic puree (see recipe)
½	Dst sp ginger puree (see recipe)
¼	Dst sp ajwain (carom) seeds, ground
1	Dst sp coriander seeds, ground
½	Dst sp cumin seeds, ground
¼	Dst sp red chilli powder
½	Dst sp tandoori masala
1	Fresh lime, juiced
2	Dst sp natural yoghurt
½	Dst sp salt

Method

1. Mix together all the marinade ingredients and marinate the chicken for a few hours.
2. Put the marinated chicken pieces on skewers and half cook over a hot charcoal grill. Alternatively, place chicken pieces on a tray in a hot oven or under a hot grill, turning over frequently, and cook until outside is burnt.
3. To make sauce, heat oil in a frying pan, add onion and half fry.
4. Add garlic, ginger, tomatoes and green chillies. Fry for a few minutes and then add a little water.
5. Add ground coriander, ground cumin, dried fenugreek leaves, almonds and pistachio nuts. Fry for a few minutes and then add a little more water.
6. Add red chilli powder, tandoori masala, turmeric powder, cream and salt and fry for a few minutes.
7. Add fresh coriander and cook for 5 minutes on low heat. Add the chicken tikka and cook for further 5 minutes. Add garam masala and serve.

Wasim Aslam, Gordon Ramsey and Mohammed Aslam receiving the Booker Prize for Excellence, Best Restaurant 2000

This is a scented and flavourful dish that is coloured by saffron. Saffron is one of the most amazing and exciting spices in the world. It is also the most precious and most expensive!

Saffron threads are the dried stigmas of Crocus Sativus Linneaus.
To gather a pound of saffron, over 200,000 stigmas must be harvested by hand, and each flower contains only three stigmas!

Luckily, only a small number of threads is needed to add saffron's distinctive yellow colour and earthy flavour. Take care when buying saffron as there are lots of cheap imitations on the market.

PILAU RICE WITH SAFFRON

Ingredients

500g	Basmati rice, washed and soaked in warm water for 20 minutes
4	Dst sp vegetable ghee
1	Medium onion, finely chopped
1	Dst sp garlic puree (see recipe)
1	Dst sp ginger puree (see recipe)
1	Tomato, diced
3	Medium cinnamon sticks, whole
4	Cloves, crushed
1	Dst sp coriander seeds, crushed
1	Dst sp cumin seeds, whole
6	Black peppercorns, whole
2	Fresh green chillies, chopped
6	Bay leaves
2	Dst sp natural yoghurt
0.5g	(Large pinch of) saffron, soaked in a little water
1	Dst sp salt

Method

1. Heat ghee in a pan and half fry onion.
2. Add garlic, ginger and tomato and fry for a few minutes. Add cumin seeds, green chillies and yoghurt and fry for a few more minutes.
3. Add cinnamon sticks, cloves, coriander seeds, black peppercorns, bay leaves and salt. Mix and fry for 1 minute.
4. Add ½ pint of water and bring to the boil. Put lid on and leave to boil for 5 minutes.
5. In a separate pan half boil rice and then drain water out.
6. Add half-boiled rice to the spice mixture and cook until the rice has absorbed all the water. Add saffron (including water) and steam cook on very low heat for half an hour. To steam cook, cover the pan with a lid wrapped in a cotton cloth and leave on a low heat. Then serve.

Sabir

*Tahir Iqbal,
manager at Shipley*

13

Gobhi with cashew nuts is a light dish with a delicate nutty flavour. To vary the spiciness of this dish, increase or reduce the garam masala, red chilli powder and dried red chillies.

14

Fresh curry leaves can be found at all good Asian shops and markets, but if you can't find them, simply soak dried curry leaves and use about 20% more.

15

This recipe originates from South India before the Mogul invasion. The Moguls introduced meat eating into old India. This is a typically beautiful Indian recipe from the vegetarian days.

13

14

15

GOBHI WITH CASHEW NUTS

Ingredients

2	Medium cauliflowers, grated (florets only, not stalks)
4	Dst sp vegetable oil
6	Dst sp garlic, crushed (or grated)
½	Dst sp ginger puree (see recipe)
3	Medium tomatoes, chopped
¼	Dst sp each of coriander seeds and cumin seeds, crushed together
1	Dst sp mustard seeds
½	Dst sp garam masala
¼	Dst sp red chilli powder
¼	Dst sp turmeric powder
4	Dried red chillies, whole
1	Handful of fresh coriander, chopped
6	Fresh curry leaves, chopped
1	Dst sp dried fenugreek leaves
10	Cashew nuts, soaked in water and then sliced
½	Dst sp salt

Method

1. Heat oil in pan and fry garlic.
2. Add ginger, tomatoes, salt and fry.
3. Add coriander seeds, cumin seeds, mustard seeds, red chillies and dried fenugreek leaves.
4. Add red chilli powder and turmeric powder and fry until spices are cooked.
5. Add grated cauliflower and curry leaves and cook on a low heat until the cauliflower has absorbed the spices and is cooked.
6. Add garam masala, fresh coriander and sliced cashew nuts and leave on a low heat for 10 minutes or until thoroughly cooked.

Strength

Varicose veins are not an uncommon outcome for people in the catering industry. We spend a lot of time on our feet, in the kitchen, standing, peeling, chopping, stirring, dishwashing, front of house, waiting, folding, listening. When I first started as a waiter in our very first restaurant in Shipley, I too spent a fair bit of time on my feet, HIDING. I was the world's worst waiter; I was so shy I did almost anything I could to stay away from having to interact with the customer. Worse still, I wasn't even paid for what I did!

Joking aside, there is a physical stamina required for this type of work. While we now employ a team of chefs and I am no longer required to stand and peel bags of onions and potatoes or to wash up, I am still happy to do it. Only last week I spent a few hours in the sink with a new member of staff, showing him not just the job but also how doing the job need not detract from one's self-esteem. Of course I also work in the offices of Aagrah and probably drive about 800 miles a week calling at the restaurants in the evenings, troubleshooting as needed, listening to staff and customers. Working 12 hours a day, 7 days a week is something many of us at Aagrah are familiar with. All in all, it can be a punishing schedule.

Mental strength has had a role to play too. In order to make something succeed you have to keep doing it, day in day out, even when the weather is bad, even if your loved ones aren't speaking to you, even when trade is poor. All of us have had to build the mental strength to withstand the pressure from the customer waiting for a meal that, for some reason or another, is in jeopardy.

The capacity to manage emotions when it all seems too much is something often learned over time. But emotional fortitude is a key quality in this industry. The support of family and staff can help, along with just good old inexorable ageing. For me and for others in my family, being so shy has probably helped because having to confront that and overcome it has set us up for managing other intense feelings.

Spiritual strength I think is an essential part of all people and something most of us share whatever our background. It's partly about knowing who you are and where you are going, if not precisely, then at least in general terms. It's the thing that keeps you upright in dark times and gives you a sense of community within your organisation and outside of it. In some ways I think it is a renewable resource. It laces Aagrah together as a firm and a family, both internally and in our connections with customers, suppliers and the community at large.

Strength comes, of course, from example. Our parents in Kashmir are one, with their immense capacity to survive conditions that most of us now will never experience. Sabir is another, with his single mindedness to provide. So too is my nephew Sajid, with his determination to survive in the teeth of so much disadvantage, such that he hung onto life until I returned from Pakistan, before choosing the day after to die. All of my family, younger members included, who have studied hard and well and not been deterred from their goals, are great examples.

Strength comes from people placing their faith in you. When I was left with our first restaurant and virtually single handedly drove it into the ground, Sabir gave me a second chance. His belief in each one of us has developed in us the strengths we now have. I hope that has allowed us, in turn, to step back and let others within Aagrah find their own strengths, which then feed into the organisation more widely. When you are running a family business, strength comes from you putting your faith in others, the older team putting faith in the younger one.

Strength has also come from our customers. Their appreciation has been an enormous source of strength to us all. Hearing how much they value our food and our service is of tremendous importance.

And over time, strength accumulates and appears to be something that can be drawn upon, like credit in a bank, whether those who have appreciated us are here or not.

قوت

19

Sabir, testing the recipes and tasting the results at Bradford College

Chicken chapari is a dry and fruity dish. The combination of savoury spices with the crushed pomegranate seeds and dried fruit creates a refreshing fusion of sweet and savoury tastes.

You should be able to find fresh curry leaves and green sultanas at all good Asian shops and markets, but if you can't, soak dried curry leaves in water, using about 20% more than fresh, and use normal sultanas.

There is no obvious substitution for pomegranate seeds (or powder). Try your local Asian shop or, failing that, try the Internet! Pomegranate seeds add a subtle sweet yet tart flavour to the dish.

CHICKEN CHANARI

Ingredients

700g	Chicken, sliced
3	Dst sp vegetable oil
1	Medium onion, chopped
6	Cloves of garlic, crushed (or grated)
1	Medium piece of ginger, peeled and crushed (or grated)
3	Medium tomatoes, chopped
½	Dst sp coriander seeds, ground
½	Dst sp cumin seeds, ground
½	Dst sp pomegranate seeds, crushed
½	Dst sp garam masala
½	Dst sp red chilli powder
½	Dst sp turmeric powder
3	Fresh green chillies, sliced
4-5	Fresh curry leaves
1	Dst sp dried fenugreek leaves
1	Handful of fresh garden mint leaves (for garnish)
4	Dried apricots, sliced
3-4	Dried plums (prunes), sliced
3	Dst sp green sultanas
½	Dst sp salt

Method

1. Heat oil and fry onions. Add garlic and ginger.
2. Add red chilli powder and turmeric powder and fry.
3. Add chicken, tomatoes, green chillies, fresh curry leaves and salt.
4. Add ground coriander, ground cumin, pomegranate seeds, garam masala, dried fenugreek leaves and dried plums and fry.
5. Add dried apricots and green sultanas. Garnish with fresh mint.

Two of the present managers at work

ZARDA (SWEET RICE)

Zarda is a sweet and fragrant dish that is at once light and filling. Even though it is sweet, zarda is often used as part of the savoury course as well as for dessert.

Try your local Asian shop or market for green sultanas and kewra (pandanus) water. Normal sultanas can be substituted for green and rose water used in place of kewra water.

In Kashmir, zarda is traditionally made for special occasions such as weddings. It is served alongside pilau rice, resulting in a heavenly mix of sweet and savoury flavours that perfectly complement the curry.

Ingredients

500g	Basmati rice, washed and soaked in warm water for 20 minutes
500g	Sugar
3	Dst sp vegetable ghee or butter
10	Green cardamoms, whole
2	Dst sp almond flakes
50g	Green sultanas
3	Dst sp kewra (pandanus) water
1g	(Large pinch of) saffron, soaked in a little water

Method

1. Boil 2 litres of water. Add soaked and drained rice and boil until just under fully cooked (should be a little firm).
2. Drain out water completely. To remove the starch present in rice, rinse with cold water.
3. Heat ghee in a pan. Add green cardamoms, sugar and a cup of water. Cook on a low heat for about 10 minutes until sugar is dissolved.
4. Add boiled and cooled rice and cook on a low heat until all water is absorbed by rice.
5. Add almond flakes and green sultanas and mix.
6. Add kewra (pandanus) water and saffron (including water). Place lid on pan and put in oven for half an hour at 120°C.

Garam masala means 'hot spice mix' in Hindi. A small quantity of this special blend of ground spices is often sprinkled over or mixed into the curry at the end of cooking to add a subtle flavour.

It is very easy to buy spices ready ground, but their shelf life is so short (around 6 months) that it is much better to grind them yourself. Whole spices retain their strength of flavour for 2-3 years if kept at room temperature.

Roasting gets rid of excess moisture (better for grinding) and releases the aromatic oils present in whole spices. Take care never to burn spices, whole or ground, as this will damage their favour and aroma.

Our parents at Garforth

GARAM MASALA

Ingredients

8	Black cardamoms (seeds only)
10	Green cardamoms, whole
5	Cinnamon sticks
10	Cloves
200g	Coriander seeds
100g	Cumin seeds
20	Black peppercorns
2	Star anise (whole star including shell)
6	Bay leaves

Method

1. Lightly roast these ingredients in an open and dry pan. Toss or move frequently to avoid burning.
2. Once cooled, grind together (using spice mill, blender, food processor or coffee grinder) and put in a jar. For longer life and aroma always replace lid after use.

CHAPPATIS

Ingredients

450g	Chappati flour
1	Litre water (this may vary)
1	Pinch of salt (optional)

Method

1. Mix flour and salt together. Add water to make a dough (not too wet, not too dry) and leave for half an hour.
2. Divide the mixture into small balls. Flour worktop and roll balls out using rolling pin. The chappatis should be circular in shape and around 15cm in diameter. Use as little flour as possible to avoid drying out the chappatis.
3. Heat a tray over a gas burner, place the chappati on the top for 30 seconds and then turn and cook other side for 30 seconds. Repeat until chappati is light brown in colour, but not too dry. Finally, expose to the naked flame to obtain further colouring (optional). The chappati should puff out when exposed to the naked flame.
4. Alternatively, place a tray directly onto an electric hob. Cook chappati on tray on a low heat, turning frequently until it puffs a little. Practice makes perfect!
5. Serve immediately.
6. This recipe makes 12 individual chappatis.

Faith

Companies are made up of people and therefore sometimes have as many different ideas and senses of direction as the number of people involved. Aagrah is no different. And when those people are also members of your family, it can be hard to fight your corner when you are sure that you should do something. It is particularly hard if it is something big, like opening another restaurant, and especially if your only justification is that you are sure it will work.

We are lucky in Aagrah, and I consider myself to be particularly lucky, that my family, older and younger members alike, have used their imagination and instinct and intuition to support me as we have grown as a company. It has meant that I have been able to push forward at times when there has been nothing concrete to give us comfort that we are doing the right thing.

I think there is a Christian saying – there is certainly an Islamic one – that says "God helps those who help themselves". It would be wrong of me to say that new ventures are the result of just having a gut feeling or a sense of surety about the success. I can use a calculator as well as anyone, and before we open a new restaurant we do crunch the numbers, look at the competition and think carefully about the market it will serve.

But when all is said and done, eventually a decision is made and, more often than not, what I call the '3 Is' have an influence. These are Imagination, Instinct and Intuition.

When I see a potential site for us I try and imagine how it would look once it is an Aagrah restaurant. I remember the Garforth site, which was originally a primary school and is the oldest building in Garforth. We thought it would make a terrific restaurant working within the existing architectural constraints. However, when local people heard that it was to be turned into a restaurant they turned up in force to protest. It was extremely gratifying to us that when they heard it was Aagrah that was undertaking the work, they went away reassured.

When we looked in Leeds we looked at a number of sites. We had already done the calculations and we knew Leeds city centre was where Aagrah needed to be. After all, we had restaurants in all the surrounding towns; it was like having the crown without the jewels. We saw several sites before we finally settled on the site at the BBC. All of the sites were appropriate; two are a stone's throw from where our Leeds restaurant now is. The costs were about the same, both for the leases and for the work that we had to do. My instincts told me that there were some real keys to success at the BBC site. It is within easy access of both the town centre and the outskirts. There is plenty of evening parking and the association with the BBC can only be good.

Intuition is something else entirely. It's the final thing that makes you choose one path over another even when all the pros and cons seem to be evenly balanced. It's the bit that is hard to articulate and for which the calculator gives no information. Sometimes in this life you just have to act on faith, to know, without evidence, what is true.

And then, of course, you hope you are right.

ایمان

27

Bihari kebab has a rather unique tangy marinade and is originally from Bihar in India. Kandhari tikka is another delicious type of kebab that uses chicken thigh for its juiciness and full flavour.

You can find crispy fried onions in most supermarkets. To make your own, salt sliced onions to remove excess liquid, dry them and fry them in oil until brown. Then leave to dry on a paper towel until crispy.

The Moguls are also responsible for the introduction of kebabs into India (along with meat). The simplicity of the preparation and cooking made them the perfect food for travelling nomads.

28

BIHARI KEBAB

Ingredients

1kg	Lamb, mini steaks or escalopes (boneless), beaten
	Vegetable oil
4	Dst sp fried onions, crushed (see filmstrip text, left)
2	Dst sp garlic puree (see recipe)
1	Dst sp ginger puree (see recipe)
1	Dst sp crushed red chilli
1	Dst sp garam masala
4	Dst sp vinegar
1	Dst sp salt

Method

1. Add appropriate quantity of oil to crushed fried onions to make a paste.
2. Mix together all the above ingredients, including fried onion paste, and allow lamb to marinate for at least 2 hours.
3. Thread marinated lamb onto flat skewers and cook over a hot charcoal grill. Alternatively, place on a tray and cook under flame or electric grill. Put as near to the heat as possible for the shortest possible time.

KANDHARI TIKKA

Ingredients

1kg	Chicken thigh, diced
2	Dst sp mustard oil
1-1½	Dst sp garlic puree (see recipe)
½	Dst sp ginger puree (see recipe)
1	Dst sp green chilli puree (see recipe)
1	Dst sp coriander seeds, crushed
½	Dst sp ground black pepper
1-1½	Dst sp pomegranate seeds, ground
1	Dst sp red chilli powder
½	Dst sp tandoori masala
2	Fresh limes, juiced
1	Pinch of saffron
1	Dst sp salt

Method

1. Mix together all the above ingredients and leave chicken to marinate in fridge for 6 hours.
2. Put marinated chicken on flat skewers and cook over a hot charcoal grill. Alternatively, place on a tray and cook under flame or electric grill. Put as near to the heat as possible for the shortest possible time, while ensuring chicken is fully cooked.

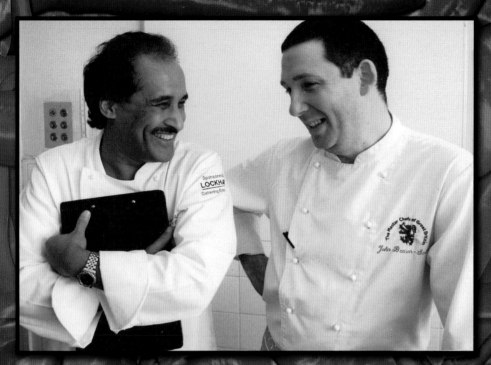

*Judges
Mohammed Aslam
and
John Benson-Smith
at the Intercollege
Competition*

Mumbai machli is a rich and flavourful fish dish. To vary the spiciness, increase or reduce the amounts of garam masala, red chilli powder, whole red chillies and yoghurt.

You may find that ajwain seeds are hard to come by. Check out your local Asian shop or market. They look like small caraway seeds and taste a little like thyme. You could always try the Internet!

Good substitutions for monkfish are coley, lobster meat or scallops. If you can't find fresh curry leaves, soak dried ones in water, using about 20% more than fresh.

MUMBAI MACHLI

Ingredients

1kg	Monkfish, cut into cubes
	Vegetable oil for deep frying
6	Dst sp olive oil
1	Medium onion, chopped
6	Cloves of garlic, crushed (or grated)
1	Dst sp ginger puree (see recipe)
3	Medium tomatoes, chopped
1	Dst sp coriander seeds, ground
½	Dst sp cumin seeds, ground
½	Dst sp garam masala
½	Dst sp red chilli powder
¼	Dst sp turmeric powder
4	Fresh red chillies, whole
6	Bay leaves
1	Handful of fresh coriander, chopped
6	Fresh curry leaves
½	Fresh lime, sliced
2	Dst sp natural yoghurt
½	Dst sp salt

Ingredients for marinade

½	Dst sp garlic puree (see recipe)
¼	Dst sp ajwain (carom) seeds, ground
1	Dst sp natural yoghurt
¼	Dst sp salt

Method

1. Marinate the fish with the ingredients shown left and deep fry until half cooked.
2. Heat olive oil in a pan and fry onion until light brown.
3. Add garlic, ginger and tomatoes and fry together with onion (for extra gravy add more onion).
4. Add yoghurt and fry for a few minutes.
5. Add red chilli powder, turmeric powder and salt.
6. Add ground coriander, ground cumin and bay leaves.
7. Add fish, garam masala, red chillies, fresh coriander and fresh curry leaves and cook gently.
8. Add lime and cook for a few minutes.

Our family at Eid feast at

home in Kashmir

in the early 1970s

32

GREEN MINT CHUTNEY

Ingredients

½	Bunch of fresh garden mint leaves
½	Dst sp coriander seeds, ground
½	Dst sp cumin seeds, ground
4	Fresh green chillies (seeds out), sliced
½	Bunch of fresh coriander
1	Dst sp lemon juice
500g	Natural yoghurt
1	Dst sp salt

Method

1. Blend together fresh mint leaves, green chillies and fresh coriander using a blender or stick blender.
2. Add this ground mixture, along with ground coriander, ground cumin, lemon juice and salt, to the yoghurt and stir or blend until a smooth consistency is achieved.
3. If the chutney is too thick, add a little milk. If it is too thin, add more yoghurt.
4. Keep refrigerated and eat within 3-4 days.

GARLIC CHUTNEY

Ingredients

5	Cloves of garlic, crushed (or grated)
1	Very small piece of ginger, crushed (or grated)
1	Medium tomato, chopped
¼	Dst sp coriander seeds, ground
¼	Dst sp cumin seeds, ground
½	Dst sp pomegranate seeds, ground
2	Fresh green chillies (seeds out), chopped
½	Handful of fresh coriander
5	Dst sp natural yoghurt
1	Pinch of salt, to taste

Method

1. Blend together all the ingredients using a blender or stick blender, until the desired consistency is achieved.
2. Keep refrigerated and eat within 3-4 days.

Green mint chutney is the yoghurt-based chutney served with poppadoms in most Asian restaurants. It is a delicious accompaniment to charcoal-grilled foods such as kebabs.

Garlic has found its way into almost every cuisine in the world. This is no bad thing as researchers believe that garlic is good for the immune system, blood pressure and in preventing heart disease.

Chutneys originate from India and are traditionally served with almost every meal; as relishes with curries and as sauces for spicy dishes (especially meats). They can be fresh or cooked. Why not try inventing your own..?

33

Communication

The name Aagrah came from us trying to spell, in English characters, a city name in India. Many people's local accents in Hindi have a short 'a' and those people would have transcribed it differently. But we have what is called 'the Persian tongue', in that our accent draws out the initial 'a' in words, hence the double 'a' at the beginning of Aagrah. Bearing in mind that at the time we could scarcely write English, let alone recite the alphabet, it is a complete fluke that this then placed Aagrah on the first pages of any alphabetical directory. However, this has been a great advantage, as any PR firm will verify. Your customer finds you fast and first.

We have been lucky at Aagrah that in the 1980s the UK mentality towards Asian cooking, and foreign foods generally, changed. The Vegetarian Society gave us our first proper review and thus communicated what we were doing to a much wider audience. And at that time we were doing something pretty unusual for the average curry house. We were using all fresh ingredients; we were blending our own spices, and had totally moved away from buying in this red sauce and this green sauce and mixing them with a few dried onions. I am exaggerating, of course, but the vast majority of curry houses at the time were still producing a hybrid curry for the English palate, and very few were using all fresh ingredients. The inclusion by Drew Smith of Aagrah in the Good Food Guide in 1982 then built on the niche market reached by the Vegetarian Society, and really put Aagrah on the map as a fine restaurant in the mainstream.

But as any business person will tell you, whatever your PR and your reviews, eventually the votes are by people with their feet. No matter what our position in the telephone directory or how many good reviews we receive, the fundamental communication is between the restaurant and the customer.

The key ingredient in this communication is respect. The onus is on the restaurant to establish a respectful atmosphere, to treat people with respect and then elicit from them the same. Ultimately, that comes from the family. If we treat each other and the people with whom we work with respect, then they communicate that to the customer.

I would say that the way in which we work with staff is more vital in creating the kind of communication that has come to be expected at Aagrah than any amount of training. We can show staff how to perform this or that task, and of course training is essential for the job, but if they have no mental awareness or feeling, then the essential part of the Aagrah experience is missing. It's like getting people to recite gormlessly after every transaction "Have a nice day now!" or "Missing you already!" Everyone knows the sentiments aren't real, and so in the end it is disrespectful all round. We try to let staff develop their own mental approach to the job by asking them really simple things like "How do you treat guests in your own home?" and telling them "That's how you need to treat Aagrah guests, only more so, because they are also paying money".

Some of what the Aagrah restaurants communicate is that they are foreign; the colours, the smells, the furniture, the service and the background chatter are all alien. And, along with the authentic nature of the Kashmiri cuisine, they carry forward the individuality of the experience throughout the meal.

But it isn't the décor that creates the atmosphere;
it is communication that underpins all we do.
To say otherwise is like mistaking the
menu for the dinner.

رابط

35

Sabir, newly arrived in the UK.
Lt Columbo...

This dish is filling and rich and the lamb exceptionally tender. The beauty of this version of pilau rice is that it is a whole meal in itself — meat and rice.

An alternative method of steam cooking is to place the pan, complete with lid, in the oven on a low heat for half an hour.

KASHMIRI PILAU RICE

Ingredients

500g	Basmati rice, washed and soaked in warm water for 20 minutes
500g	Lamb chops
4	Dst sp vegetable ghee or butter
2	Dst sp vegetable oil
1	Medium onion, sliced
4	Cloves of garlic, peeled and chopped
1	Medium tomato, chopped
6	Green cardamoms, crushed
2	Medium cinnamon sticks, whole
4	Cloves, crushed
8	Black peppercorns, crushed
2	Fresh green chillies, chopped
4-6	Bay leaves
25g	Almond flakes
2	Cooking apples, sliced
25g	Green sultanas
2	Dst sp rose water
1g	(Large pinch of) saffron, soaked in a little water
1	Dst sp salt

Method

1. Heat oil in a pan. Wash the lamb chops and cook until tender on a low heat with ½ the onion, 2 cloves of garlic, 4 green cardamoms, cinnamon sticks, cloves, black peppercorns, bay leaves and ½ dessertspoon of salt. Then separate meat from sauce.

2. Heat 3 dessertspoons of ghee in a pan, add remaining ½ onion and fry until light brown. Add remaining 2 cloves of garlic, tomato and green chillies and fry for a few minutes.

3. Add lamb chops and keep on frying until colour of chops becomes light brown. Add sauce (and spices) from chops and 1½ pints of water. Bring to the boil and allow to boil for 5 minutes.

4. Add soaked and drained rice, remaining ½ dessertspoon of salt and boil until rice absorbs all the water. Add almond flakes, green sultanas, rose water and saffron (including water) and steam cook for about half an hour. To steam cook, cover the pan with a lid wrapped in a cotton cloth and leave on a low heat.

5. Heat remaining dessertspoon of ghee in a pan. Add remaining 2 green cardamoms, wait a few moments, then add and sauté the sliced cooking apples.

6. Spread apple on top of rice before serving.

When buying saffron, make sure you buy saffron threads, not powder, and that they are red in colour with a slightly orange tip. The powder is easier to fake than the threads, and if the threads are entirely red they may have been dyed.

Saag dall is a satisfying lentil and spinach dish. It can be served as a side dish or as a main course. To make it vegan, simply substitute the yoghurt for a little (very little) water.

You may struggle to find fresh fenugreek (methi). Dried is much easier to get hold of and is a good substitute for fresh. Yellow split lentils, which look like chickpeas split in half, are a good substitute for green lentils (moong).

There is no substitute for asafoetida (hing) powder, but you should be able to find it in supermarkets, Asian shops and some health sto It is one of the strongest spices in the world a is thought to counter flatulence...!

Sabir with staff at Pudsey

SAAG DALL

Ingredients

100g	Green lentils (moong), washed and soaked in warm water for half an hour
2	Bunches of spring spinach, thoroughly washed and chopped
4	Dst sp vegetable oil
1	Small onion, finely sliced
2	Dsp sp garlic puree (see recipe)
1	Large tomato, cut into small cubes
2	Green cardamoms, crushed
2	Medium cinnamon sticks, crushed
1	Dst sp coriander seeds, ground
½	Dst sp cumin seeds, ground
½	Dst sp asafoetida powder
1	Dst sp garam masala
½	Dst sp red chilli powder
¼	Dst sp turmeric powder
2	Fresh green chillies, chopped
1	Handful of fresh coriander, chopped
1	Bunch of fresh fenugreek leaves (whole leaves only)
2	Dst sp natural yoghurt
1	Dst sp salt

Method

1. Heat oil in a pan.
2. Add onion and fry until light brown.
3. Add garlic, tomato, asafoetida powder and green chillies and fry for a few minutes. Add yoghurt and fry for a few more minutes.
4. Add green cardamoms, cinnamon sticks, ground coriander, ground cumin, garam masala, red chilli powder, turmeric powder and salt and cook for about 5 minutes.
5. Add spinach and fresh fenugreek leaves and stir to coat all leaves with the spices.
6. Add soaked and drained lentils and a cup of water. Stir and cook on a low heat until the lentils are cooked.
7. Add fresh coriander. Increase the heat and keep stirring until the dish becomes dry.

This dish is savoury and full of flavour. The combination of spices, meat, vegetables and seasonings makes for a beautifully balanced chicken curry. The pickled garlic is the key to this dish.

You can find fried onions ready fried and crispy in packets in most good supermarkets. To vary the spiciness of this dish, increase or decrease the levels of garam masala, red chilli powder and green chillies.

Turmeric powder is used in most curry recipes. It adds colour and flavour to the dish but the main reason it is used so frequently is because it acts as an antidote to chilli. It is also a skin softener and is wound cleansing.

Sabir and Richard Whiteley

LAHSEN CHICKEN

Ingredients

1kg	Boneless chicken, sliced
6	Dst sp olive oil
1	Medium onion, sliced
4	Dst sp fried onions (for garnish)
4	Dst sp garlic puree (see recipe)
1	Medium piece of ginger, peeled and crushed (or grated)
3	Medium tomatoes, chopped
3-4	Green cardamoms, crushed
½	Dst sp coriander seeds, ground
½	Dst sp cumin seeds, ground
½	Dst sp garam masala
½	Dst sp red chilli powder
½	Dst sp turmeric powder
4-6	Fresh green chillies, chopped
1	Handful of fresh coriander, chopped
6	Fresh curry leaves
2	Dst sp dried fenugreek leaves
½	Fresh lime, sliced
1	Red pepper, sliced
1½	Dst sp garlic pickle
½	Dst sp sugar
½	Dst sp salt

Method

1. Heat oil and fry garlic and ginger.
2. Add chicken, red chilli powder, turmeric powder, garlic pickle and salt and cook on a high heat for 2 minutes.
3. Add onion, tomatoes, green chillies, lime and red pepper.
4. Add green cardamoms, ground coriander, ground cumin, garam masala, dried fenugreek leaves and sugar.
5. Add fresh coriander and fresh curry leaves and serve.
6. Garnish with fried onions.

Fear

There's nothing quite like a healthy dose of fear to keep you sharp and safe. It makes you question what you are doing and the wisdom of the course you have set yourself.

We have had moments of real fear during the life of Aagrah. The most notable was in 1987 when we had two restaurants in the group, one in Pudsey and one in Shipley.

I personally was running the restaurant in Pudsey. My brother Sabir was away on Haj. It was the day after Eid al Adha – Day of Sacrifice – when we had a visit from an officer of the Environmental Health Department. Some customers had complained of food poisoning following a meal in the restaurant and they had come to investigate.

At the time, I knew nothing of the procedures involved in following up complaints from the public. I didn't know that there needed to be evidence linking the food poisoning to a particular source, and that the public can't simply point a finger and take successful legal action without having some proof to back it up. I was just terrified. I asked the officer what action he recommended and then we took it. In fact, he did not ask us to close the restaurant, but, to satisfy myself and to ensure that no chances were taken with the health of the public, I did so. We closed, disinfected from top to bottom, threw all the food away and started afresh. To my horror, I then found that what was meant to have been a confidential inspection had been leaked to the press.

Sabir returned from Haj on the second day we were closed, and of course asked how the restaurant was doing. I burst into tears and told him all. He was satisfied with the way we had handled things, and the following day we re-opened.

It turned out to have been a false alarm, and the Environmental Health issued us with a clean bill of health. Despite my fears, within two days of re-opening Pudsey, we were full again every night. Our customers had not believed the reports. I still find that remarkable. They were a tower of strength for Aagrah.

But the whole experience did alert us to the training opportunities available, and we sent staff and ourselves on all the available courses.

When the Choice awards were opened for nominations the Environmental Health Department suggested we apply, and Aagrah was the first restaurant to win the annual award.

43

LULU

44

NAN BREAD

Interestingly, in Asia, curry is intended solely as flavour to accompany rice and breads, whereas in the UK it is served as the main meal. Perhaps this is why curry has a reputation in the UK of being unhealthy! As with any foods, care should always be taken not to consume in excess.

Nan bread is an Asian flatbread that traditionally accompanies curries. Onion seeds (also called nigella and black caraway) contribute to the distinctive flavour of these flatbreads and aid digestion.

In Asia, nan breads are cooked in a tandoor, which is a charcoal-fired, barrel-shaped clay oven. The breads are stuck to the thick walls of the tandoor and cook very quickly due to high temperatures of up to 250°C!

Ingredients

1kg	Self raising flour
	Vegetable oil for cooking
1	Dst sp onion seeds
1	Egg
½	Pint milk mixed with ½ pint water
1	Dst sp natural yoghurt
½	Dst sp baking powder
1	Dst sp sugar
1	Pinch of salt, to taste

Method

1. Mix together all the above ingredients (except oil) to form a dough. Leave in bowl for 1 hour.
2. Brush oil onto baking tray. Divide the mixture and make into balls. Place the balls on the tray.
3. Cover with cling film or cloths covered with oil on the underside, so that all surfaces of the balls of dough are coated in oil. Leave for 1 hour.
4. Spread oil on worktop (do not use flour), flatten dough balls on worktop and work with hands to create rounded shape of nan breads.
5. Heat tawa (flat tray) under grill. When hot, place nan on tawa (no oil necessary) and cook under the hot grill.
6. It is not necessary to turn the nan over because, as the grill cooks the top, the base is being baked by the heat of the tray. (If you have a tandoor, apply nans on its walls and they should be cooked in around 3 minutes.)
7. When brown in colour, brush margarine on the nan (optional) and serve.
8. This recipe makes 6 good-sized nans.

46

Future manager...

Gosht achar is a dry, aromatic dish. This recipe was among those that won Aagrah director, Mohammed Aslam, the International Chef of the Year competition in Edinburgh, 1996.

This dish is a favourite in Central India and can be made with chicken, but red meat is more suitable for use with pickled spices. To make the dish dairy-free, simply avoid the yoghurt.

Achar means pickle and in this recipe refers to the combination of different seeds with yoghurt and vinegar. You can add ready-made mixed pickle instead, but using fresh seeds ensures a much more delicious and unusual flavour.

GOSHT ACHAR

Ingredients

1kg	Boneless lamb, cut into cubes
6	Dst sp vegetable oil
1	Medium onion, chopped
2	Dst sp garlic puree (see recipe)
1	Dst sp ginger puree (see recipe)
3	Medium tomatoes, chopped
3-4	Green cardamoms, whole
1	Dst sp coriander seeds, ground
½	Dst sp cumin seeds, ground
½	Dst sp fennel seeds
½	Dst sp fenugreek seeds
½	Dst sp mustard seeds
½	Dst sp onion seeds
½	Dst sp garam masala
1	Dst sp red chilli powder
¼	Dst sp turmeric powder
4-5	Fresh green chillies, whole
6	Bay leaves
1	Handful of fresh coriander, chopped
2	Dst sp natural yoghurt
1	Dst sp white vinegar
½	Dst sp salt

Method

1. Heat oil, add onion and fry until light brown.
2. Add garlic, ginger and tomatoes and fry together with onion.
3. Add lamb and salt and cook until lamb is tender.
4. Add green cardamoms, fennel seeds, fenugreek seeds, mustard seeds, onion seeds and bay leaves and cook for a good few minutes. Then add yoghurt and vinegar.
5. Add ground coriander, ground cumin, red chilli powder, turmeric powder and green chillies and stir until spices are fully cooked.
6. Add fresh coriander and cook for a few minutes.
7. Sprinkle with garam masala and serve.

47

Described by some as a 'fancy rice casserole', this traditional rice and chicken dish is delightfully aromatic and is a complete meal in itself. To make it dairy-free, simply replace the yoghurt and milk with water.

Along with many other dishes and traditions, the biryani dish is thought to have arrived in Asia from the Middle East. Many people believe that biryani originates from the Persian word 'birian', which means 'fried before cooking'.

The biryani is such a popular dish that each region and province and even community has developed its own version. Some have even made it their life's work to document the origin of each biryani along with the different traditions involved in making them!

Wasim Aslam, Young Entrepreneur Award

MURGH BIRYANI

Ingredients

500g	Chicken, on or off the bone, washed and cut into medium pieces	¼	Dst sp nutmeg, ground (or grated)
4-6	Dst sp vegetable oil	4-6	Fresh green chillies, sliced
½	Small onion, sliced	8	Bay leaves
1	Dst sp garlic puree (see recipe)	1	Handful of fresh coriander, chopped
½	Dst sp ginger puree (see recipe)	12	Leaves of fresh garden mint
1	Medium piece of ginger, sliced	6-8	Dried plums (prunes), stoned and sliced
6	Medium tomatoes, chopped	4	Dst sp natural yoghurt
4	Green cardamoms, ground	1	Dst sp salt
1	Dst sp crushed red chilli		
1	Medium cinnamon stick, whole		
4	Cloves, crushed		
1	Dst sp coriander seeds, ground		
1	Dst sp cumin seeds, ground		
8	Black peppercorns, crushed		
½	Dst sp amchoor (mango powder)		
¼	Dst sp mace, ground		

Ingredients for rice

500g	Basmati rice, washed and soaked in warm water for 45 minutes
1	Fresh lime, peeled and sliced
1	Cup of milk
4	Dst sp kewra (pandanus) water
1	Pinch of saffron
2	Dst sp salt

Method

1. Heat oil in pan. Add onion and fry until light brown. Add garlic and ginger (puree) and fry for a few minutes.
2. Add chicken and fry until sealed.
3. Add ground coriander, ground cumin, amchoor (mango powder), green chillies and bay leaves and fry for 1 minute.
4. Add sliced ginger, tomatoes, green cardamoms, crushed red chilli, cinnamon stick, cloves, black peppercorns, mace, nutmeg, dried plums, yoghurt and 1 dessertspoon of salt. Cook for a good few minutes. Add fresh coriander and fresh mint and stir. Keep to one side.
5. Heat milk. Soak saffron in hot milk for 15 minutes.
6. Boil 4 litres of water in a large pan. Add 2 dessertspoons of salt. Add soaked and drained rice and boil until rice is just over half cooked. Drain all water out and put rice back in pan.
7. Spread chicken mixture on top of rice. Pour the milk (with saffron) and kewra (pandanus) water evenly over the whole dish. Sprinkle lime slices on the top.
8. Preheat oven to 120°C. Place lid on pan and put in oven for half an hour. Ensure chicken is thoroughly cooked before serving.

Humour

Every industry has its humour. Catering is no exception. The places you need it most are in the kitchen and in the toilets. Not the staff toilets, by the way, but the ones used by the public...

I can remember when we opened in Garforth. The restaurant had been running for some months when a young member of staff came and reported to me the state of the gents' toilets. I won't describe what greeted me when I went through the door. Anyone who has worked in nursing or the licensed trade will have met such sights many times. But this poor lad was horrified. So I sent him to find me some rubber gloves and set to on my knees to dislodge the blockage and then mop up the debris. By the time I had finished, with him looking on, I had gone from somewhat frightening employer to living saint, neither of which was a true image. I said to him, removing my gloves as I did so, "Look, my hands and arms are still here! I am still the same person!" And he laughed. That was good.

In 1989 I took an order for an outside catering event for 150 people in Huddersfield. I took the order six months in advance, and, as the day approached, I noticed to my horror that it fell on Eid, which, like Easter, is a lunar feast and so its date changes from year to year. Seeing as Eid is as important in our calendar as Christmas Day is in the UK, I could not possibly ask anyone to work. So I rang the cutomer to confirm that that in fact was the day, hoping, I suppose, that there might be some mistake or margin for manoeuvre. Not a bit of it. Guests were travelling half way across the world for the event and the food had to be there. So I duly set to work the day before and worked all through the night to complete the order. One of my nephews took pity on me I think, and very kindly drove it all to Huddersfield. I asked him when he returned if the event was going well. He said to me "Cha cha. The food is there. That's our part of the bargain. The rest is up to them. Now let's go home and have Eid".

In one of our restaurants we had a large potted plant that periodically went missing. Over the years, we replaced that plant quite a few times. Then, one evening, a gang of lads came in after the pub for a curry. They were regular customers who often came to eat late in the evening. As they left, a young woman who had been seated at the bar came over to me and said that she didn't know whether I had noticed, but she thought the group of men had taken the large pot plant. The next time the young men came in, I called the offender over to the bar and invited him to a beer on the house, and fell to chatting with him about this and that. I asked him if he and his friends enjoyed coming to the restaurant and he said that they did. So I enquired gently as to why then he had taken the pot plant. He looked sheepish, apologised and then went to join his habitual friends for their meal.

The following week, a very sleek vehicle pulled up outside, driven by one of the young men who had been in the group. Very apologetically, he retrieved the pot plant from the back of the vehicle, then another, and another. We had no room to put them in the restaurant! To my delight, these young men still come to the restaurant, not so young and not so late at night after the pub, but with their wives and children, and we still have a good laugh about the plants.

Just last month, we were a driver short at the central kitchen, and I was around with nothing pressing so I jumped in and took the delivery to Leeds. When I arrived, the restaurant was not yet open and no members of staff were on site, but someone from the BBC centre, located above us, approached me and asked if he could speak to the manager. I said that the manager had not yet arrived but he could speak to me if he wished. He said no, he needed to talk to a senior member of staff. I laughed and said "Well, I am the MD, I just happen to be driving a truck today..." So of course we talked. It's always worth remembering that jobs are what people do, and not who they are.

مزاح

51

Two ruffians at large...

Fish balti is a light, wet dish. The famous balti tradition originates from the North-West Frontier Province of Pakistan.

Baltis are a great choice for tribesmen and gypsies because you cook and eat out of the same dish. You can even cook flatbreads on the underside of the balti dish.

FISH BALTI

Ingredients

1kg	Cod (or monkfish to avoid excessive flaking), sliced
3	Dst sp olive oil
4	Dst sp garlic puree (see recipe)
2	Dst sp ginger puree (see recipe)
5	Medium tomatoes, cut into wedge shape
2	Dst sp coriander seeds, ground
1	Dst sp cumin seeds, ground
1	Dst sp red chilli powder
½	Dst sp turmeric powder
5	Fresh green chillies, sliced
2	Handfuls of fresh coriander, chopped
½	Dst sp salt

Method

1. Heat olive oil in large balti dish.
2. Add garlic and ginger and stir constantly over a high heat.
3. Add ground coriander, ground cumin, red chilli powder, turmeric powder and salt and stir.
4. Add fish slices and mix with the spices. To avoid flaking of fish, either fry first and then mix with spices or mix carefully with spatula.
5. Add green chillies.
6. Once the oil, spices and juices from the fish have been absorbed, add the tomatoes.
7. Add fresh coriander and stir. Put a lid on the balti and leave over a medium heat until fish is thoroughly cooked. Allow to simmer for a while.

Baltis are very simple and quick to make once you've learnt the formula. To make chicken or lamb balti, simply add the meat to the oil, then add garlic and ginger and follow the remaining fish balti instructions.

Nikon D70 DIGITAL IMAGE

iNovaChrome · 37 ·

53

Traditional dag or cooking pots

This is a very rich and aromatic dish with a full flavour that is intensified by the addition of bones of lamb shank.

The title of this recipe refers to a type of cooking pot. Kunnas are clay pots mostly used in Punjab, especially at parties. The kunna is traditionally cooked on a charcoal fireplace half buried in the ground.

If you prefer, you can substitute the butter for vegetable ghee or oil. Also, the amounts of crushed red chilli, black peppercorns, garam masala and green chillies can be varied to make the dish more or less spicy.

KUNNA GOSHT

Ingredients

1kg	Boneless lamb, cut into large pieces
2	Medium bones of lamb shank
200g	Butter
½	Medium onion, sliced and lightly fried (for garnish)
12	Cloves of garlic, crushed (or grated)
¼	Small piece of ginger, sliced (for garnish)
5	Medium tomatoes, chopped
4	Black cardamoms, whole
1	Dst sp crushed red chilli
2	Medium cinnamon sticks, whole
4	Cloves, crushed
1	Dst sp coriander seeds, crushed
½	Dst sp cumin seeds, ground
1	Dst sp black cumin seeds (or dried fenugreek leaves), crushed between palms (for garnish)
½	Dst sp black peppercorns, crushed
1	Dst sp garam masala
¼	Dst sp mace, ground
½	Dst sp nutmeg, ground (or grated)
½	Dst sp turmeric powder
3	Fresh green chillies, chopped (for garnish)
6	Bay leaves
1	Handful of fresh coriander (for garnish)
½	Dst sp salt, or to taste

Method

1. Boil ½ litre of water and add black cardamoms, cinnamon sticks and bay leaves. Allow to boil gently for 15-20 minutes.
2. Heat butter in kunna if available. Alternatively, use a deep pan with a thick base.
3. Add boneless lamb and lamb shanks and fry until sealed.
4. Add garlic, tomatoes, crushed red chilli, cloves, coriander seeds, ground cumin, black peppercorns, garam masala, mace, nutmeg, turmeric powder and salt. Fry for 5 minutes.
5. Add spiced water (discard whole spices) and bring to the boil. Cover the pan with a lid wrapped in a damp cotton cloth and cook for about 1 hour on a low heat. Do not add any additional water as lamb should cook in its own juice.
6. Sprinkle fried onion, sliced ginger, black cumin seeds (or dried fenugreek leaves), green chillies and fresh coriander on top as garnish and cover with lid for 10 minutes.
Serve with chappatis.

Our kitchens; note the clay oven or tandoor

This mushroom recipe is a lovely fusion of fresh, tart flavours. If using king prawns in the prawn dish, slice into 4 and dip in the spicy batter. The prawns will then open when cooked..

Sesame seeds are a lovely addition to the prawn recipe as they contribute a mild, nutty flavour and a delicate crunch. They are also a good source of important nutrients and are thought to be the oldest condiment known to man!

To make the mushroom dish vegan and gluten-free, simply grill without adding the cheese or breadcrumbs. Using rice flour instead of wheat flour in makrani jhinga gives a crispy effect and will make the dish gluten-free.

STUFFED OVEN~BAKED MUSHROOM

Ingredients

4	Large mushrooms
½	Onion, chopped
2	Medium tomatoes, chopped
1	Dst sp cumin seeds, crushed
1	Dst sp pomegranate seeds, crushed
4	Fresh green chillies, chopped
1	Handful of fresh coriander, chopped
1	Lemon, juiced
	Grated cheese or breadcrumbs for topping
¼	Dst sp salt

Method

1. Remove the skin from the mushrooms. Scoop out the stem and mushroom from inside and chop into small pieces.
2. Mix the onion, tomatoes, cumin seeds, pomegranate seeds, green chillies, fresh coriander, lemon juice and salt with the chopped mushroom mixture and stuff back into mushroom shells. Place stuffed mushrooms on an oiled tray.
3. Sprinkle the cheese or breadcrumbs onto mushrooms, then place them in oven or under grill for 15 minutes, or until cooked.

MAKRANI JHINGA

Ingredients

500g	Prawn tails, cooked and peeled
	Vegetable oil for deep frying

Ingredients for batter

250g	Wheat flour
2	Dst sp vegetable oil
1	Dst sp garlic puree (see recipe)
1	Dst sp green chilli puree (see recipe)
½	Dst sp sesame seeds
3	Dst sp lime juice
1	Egg
1	Cup of water
¼	Dst sp salt

Method

1. Mix together all the batter ingredients except oil.
2. Heat the 2 dessertspoons of oil in a pan and add to the batter. Mix and leave for 20 minutes.
3. Heat enough vegetable oil in a pan for deep frying. Dip prawns in batter and deep fry until light brown.
4. Serve with tamarind chutney (see recipe) or a chutney of your choice.

Loss

When I think back over the years of striving, I am aware that a lot of things were cast on the sacrificial fire of success.

Probably the largest and most acute loss for me has been my family life with my wife and children. I cannot remember when I last had real time off. Of course I have hours here and there, but the luxury of unscheduled days stretching out before me has yet to come. This has meant not just that I have not had time off myself, but neither has my immediate family. They too have always been under the gun of my schedule and at the mercy of my drive towards improving the company. Some things inevitably get lost in the inexorable grind of creating and serving thousands of meals per day. And, naturally, some of the things lost cannot even be described.

In my immediate family, we probably each have private and unspoken grief about the costs I incurred for us all. I have been very fortunate in my life partner as she has understood that running our successful family business could only happen if she was prepared to run the home. We have always set our goals and concentrated on achieving them, not just for ourselves but for the family as a whole, in its broadest sense. It doesn't matter who gets what, since as long as the benefits come, everyone gains in the long run.

And then of course there are the losses we have in the course of any life, which sadden us, slow us, unite us and give us new perspectives. The death of Sajid, my nephew, I have spoken about already, and the influence that this has had on the development of the restaurants and on us as a team. I think also the loss of my father was huge. I miss him still.

We boys, who left the native land so young and took on so much, lost our childhood I suppose. This is particularly true for Sabir, who in the end virtually brought up Zafar and me, and therefore had a father's responsibilities at a very young age.

And in a sense I think I lost my mother. By that I mean through not living with her, I lost the habit of her; I still find it hard to call out to her as a son to a mother.

And there have been other unexpected losses. Most dramatically, there was the arson attack on the Pudsey branch, when the entire restaurant was gutted with huge financial losses. Fire is a swift and dramatic destroyer of life and property and is as frightening as any natural phenomenon. As sudden and as rapid as the damage was, we were fortunate in the speed with which we were able to recover and re-open the site. We were also fortunate to have staff team members who were such pillars of support.

More recently, my own health has given me cause for concern and I have felt, to some extent, the loss of my own sense of invincibility. But Aagrah remains strong in itself as a platform for all of us, and so, while some things seem to have been given up, a great deal has been gained.

نقصان

59

Mr Mohammed Aslam being presented with
the Best Entrepreneur plaque by
Mr Loyd Grossman in March 1996

This is a dry dish, traditionally served with nan bread or chappatis. Bhindi piaz is lovely as an accompaniment to a meal or as a whole meal in itself.

Okra, intriguingly also known as ladies fingers, is thought to be of African origin. Whilst fairly absent from the British kitchen, the pods of the okra plant are a widely eaten delicacy in South Asia.

Don't cook okra with water because this will cause the pods to become slimy. The best way is to dry fry for a short time or until crispy. To make this dish vegan, simply substitute the yoghurt for a little lime juice.

BHINDI PIAZ

Ingredients

450g	Fresh okra, cut into medium pieces
½	Cup of vegetable oil
2	Medium onions, chopped
6	Cloves of garlic, crushed (or grated)
1	Medium piece of ginger, peeled and crushed (or grated)
4	Medium tomatoes, chopped
4	Green cardamoms, crushed
2	Medium cinnamon sticks, whole
1	Dst sp coriander seeds, ground
1	Dst sp cumin seeds, ground
1	Dst sp pomegranate seeds, ground
½	Dst sp red chilli powder
½	Dst sp turmeric powder
3-4	Fresh green chillies, chopped
4-6	Bay leaves
1	Handful of fresh coriander, chopped
1	Dst sp dried fenugreek leaves
2	Dst sp natural yoghurt

Method

1. Heat ½ the oil in a pan, stir fry the okra and keep to one side.
2. Heat remaining oil and fry onion, garlic and ginger.
3. Add tomatoes, green cardamoms, cinnamon sticks, ground coriander, ground cumin, ground pomegranate seeds, green chillies, bay leaves, dried fenugreek leaves and yoghurt and cook for a few minutes.
4. Add the fried okra, red chilli powder, turmeric powder and fresh coriander and leave over heat until the spices are properly cooked.

61

Aagrah kids at Bradford Festival

Zafrani korma is a rich and scented dish from Kashmir. Unlike the generally accepted version of korma, this is a drier chicken dish whose rich flavour and aromatic spices are not overshadowed by excess sauce.

Korma refers to a style of cooking in which dairy products and often nuts are used. Although kormas are thought to be rich and fattening, you can see from this recipe that a korma needn't be full of calories.

You can vary the fat content of this dish as well as its spiciness. You can add more or less oil and yoghurt and you can vary the quantities of hot spices; garam masala, ground pepper, red chilli powder and fresh red chillies.

ZAFRANI KORMA (KASHMIRI)

Ingredients

1kg	Chicken breast, diced
6	Dst sp vegetable oil
1	Large onion, finely chopped
2	Dst sp garlic puree (see recipe)
1	Dst sp ginger puree (see recipe)
4	Green cardamoms, ground with cinnamon
1	Medium cinnamon stick, ground with cardamom
½	Dst sp coriander seeds, ground
½	Dst sp cumin seeds, ground
½	Dst sp garam masala
¼	Dst sp ground black pepper
1	Dst sp red chilli powder
½	Dst sp turmeric powder
5	Fresh red chillies, whole
4	Bay leaves
1	Pinch of fresh coriander, chopped
½	Dst sp dried fenugreek leaves
6	Leaves of fresh garden mint (for garnish)
1	Dst sp green sultanas
4	Dst sp natural yoghurt
2	Dst sp kewra (pandanus) water
1	Pinch of saffron, soaked in ½ cup water
½	Dst sp salt

Method

1. Heat oil and add onion. Fry until light brown.
2. Add garlic and ginger and fry for 5 minutes.
3. Add chicken, turmeric powder, red chillies and salt and fry until chicken is sealed.
4. Add red chilli powder and cook for a few minutes.
5. Add yoghurt and cook for 2 minutes.
6. Add ground cardamoms and cinnamon stick, ground coriander, ground cumin, garam masala, black pepper, bay leaves and dried fenugreek leaves and stir until spices and chicken are cooked.
7. Add fresh coriander, sultanas, kewra water and saffron (including water) and mix.
8. Garnish with fresh mint and serve.

63

13

Spicy fillet of salmon is a healthy, succulent and tender dish with a full, yet fresh flavour. Chop piaz is cooked like a stir fry, creating lamb chops that will melt in your mouth.

13

13

In chop piaz, as with many Asian dishes, there is a point, once the spices have been cooked, when the oil separates from the dish. The excess oil then can and should be removed. This will make the dish healthier, without ruining the flavour.

13

14

The tomato is an integral part of the culinary endeavours of multiple cultures and has worked its way into thousands of recipes across many cuisines. Asian food is no exception. Almost every recipe in this book uses a tomato or 2!

14

SPICY FILLET OF SALMON

Ingredients

500g	Salmon fillets
4	Dst sp olive oil
1	Dst sp garlic puree (see recipe)
1	Small piece of ginger, grated
4-6	Fresh or tinned plum tomatoes, boiled, peeled and mashed
4-6	Dried red chillies, whole
1	Pinch of fresh coriander
½	Dst sp dried fenugreek leaves
¼	Dst sp salt

Ingredients for marinade

2	Dst sp olive oil
1	Dst sp garlic puree (see recipe)
¼	Dst sp ajwain (carom) seeds, ground
¼	Dst sp coriander seeds, ground
¼	Dst sp cumin seeds, ground
¼	Dst sp red chilli powder
½	Fresh lime, juiced
¼	Dst sp salt

Method

1. Mix together all the marinade ingredients and marinate salmon for at least 2 hours.
2. To make sauce, heat oil in a pan, add garlic and fry until light brown.
3. Add ginger and red chillies and stir fry for half a minute.
4. Add tomatoes, fresh coriander, dried fenugreek leaves and salt. Stir fry using a little water if needed.
5. Place marinated salmon on a tray lined with tin foil and grill until fully cooked.
6. Pour spicy sauce over salmon and serve.

CHOP PIAZ

Ingredients

8 -10	Lamb chops
4	Dst sp vegetable oil
1	Medium onion, sliced
2	Spring onions (including green ends), chopped
3	Fresh green chillies, chopped
1	Handful of fresh coriander, chopped
6	Fresh curry leaves
6	Leaves of fresh garden mint
1	Fresh lime, juiced
¼	Dst sp salt

Ingredients for marinade

2	Dst sp mustard oil
1	Dst sp garlic puree (see recipe)
¼	Dst sp coriander seeds, ground
¼	Dst sp cumin seeds, ground
¼	Dst sp red chilli powder
½	Fresh lime, juiced
¼	Dst sp salt

Method

1. Marinate chops with the ingredients shown below.
2. Heat oil in non-stick pan and shallow fry all chops. Turn them over on a low heat until they are light brown. Make sure that spices do not get burnt.
3. Add onion, green chillies and salt and cook for a few minutes with lid on.
4. Add spring onions, fresh coriander, fresh curry leaves and fresh mint and stir fry.
5. Reduce the heat and cover with lid. Leave for 5 minutes.
6. Add lime juice and serve.

Responsibility

People sometimes ask me about my faith as a Muslim, and it may seem strange that I discuss it here in the context of responsibility. But, for me, that is what being a Muslim is all about – my responsibility towards God, and my responsibility towards people.

Just in case this sounds a bit pompous, my relationship with God is nobody's business but mine and His. I am not about to discuss it here or anywhere else.

My responsibilities to people are another thing altogether, and this has been played out in many ways – with the staff and the family, between the staff and the family, between the staff, between the older and the younger members of the family and so on.

And that is just within the Aagrah group.

Externally, of course, there have also been the responsibilities we believe we have to our customers, and our suppliers, and to the communities within which we trade. To some extent this explains the Aagrah commitment to charity work. In 1979 we made a commitment to fund an eye hospital in Pakistan which we have continued to the present day, at the same time as devoting half of our charitable efforts to UK organisations.

In business overall, the usual words of wisdom apply: rip no-one off.

In the restaurant trade, that means using the best and freshest ingredients. If it does not sell, don't serve it the next day; if you run out, say so, and don't try and cobble together more.

It also means paying the staff well, treating them as part of the family, with dignity. That's why I say Aagrah is one big happy family. That's how we run the group.

Finally, it means taking responsibility for offering true hospitality to people. After all, this is called the 'hospitality industry'. Ultimately, this must mean being prepared to extend to others the same freedoms we enjoy ourselves, by not being judgemental about what people drink, eat or smoke. So what if they wear different clothes, observe different traditions, pray to other gods? In the end, taking responsibility for who we are ourselves should mean that we can easily sit at table and enjoy the company of people who are different without it being threatening to us.

Actually, if I take care of my responsibilities towards people, the chances are that a lot of my responsibilities towards God will also be taken care of...

ذمہ داری

67

The combination of fish and spiced vegetables in this dish ensures a perfect balance of flavours and the steam method of cooking guarantees that the fish will be moist and tender.

Ajwain is a popular spice in Asia and is used mostly in fish and curry dishes. It is thought to reduce leftover fish smells! Unfortunately, ajwain seeds can be hard to find and there is no ideal substitute. Try your local Asian shop or market, or even the Internet!

Most households, however, will have ajwain seeds, not just for their culinary purposes, but also for their supposed medicinal properties. Ajwain is considered to be an effective medicine for treating indigestion and is often swallowed with water like tablets!

Another future manager...

PAN~BAKED SPICED FISH

Ingredients

500g	Fish (salmon, cod or haddock), sliced
2	Dst sp olive oil
2	Medium onions, chopped
3	Medium tomatoes, cut into small pieces
1	Dst sp ajwain (carom) seeds
1	Dst sp coriander seeds, ground
1	Dst sp cumin seeds, ground
1	Dst sp pomegranate seeds, ground
3	Fresh green chillies, finely chopped
1	Handful of fresh coriander, chopped
1	Fresh lime, juiced
¼	Each of red, green and yellow peppers, chopped
1	Dst sp salt

Method

1. Sprinkle the ajwain (carom) seeds and salt on the fish and gently rub. Leave for 10 minutes.
2. Mix together thoroughly in a bowl the oil, onions, tomatoes, ground coriander, ground cumin, ground pomegranate seeds, green chillies, fresh coriander, lime juice and peppers.
3. Put tin foil in a shallow tray and spread some of the mixture on it.
4. Put fish on top and spread remaining mixture over and around the fish. Cover and wrap with tin foil.
5. Preheat oven to 180°C and place tray in oven to steam cook for approximately 30-40 minutes.

Sabir and a friend

It really is worth taking the time to make garlic and ginger puree if you are planning on making more than one or two curries. You will save yourself so much hassle in the long run!

Removing the seeds from chillies and the flesh that holds the seeds in place will reduce the spiciness of these capsicum fruits. Remember not to touch delicate parts of the body after handling chillies!

GARLIC PUREE

Ingredients

250g   Fresh garlic, peeled
       (4-6 whole bulbs)
4   Dst sp vegetable oil (quantity of
       oil can be increased/reduced as
       required)

Method

1.   Using a blender or stick blender,
     combine both ingredients to make
     a puree.
2.   Put in a jar or tub with lid on.
3.   Keep in fridge. Preferably use
     within 3 weeks.

GINGER PUREE

Ingredients

250g   Fresh ginger, peeled and cut into small
       pieces (6-8 medium pieces)
4   Dst sp vegetable oil (quantity of oil can be
       increased/reduced as required)

Method

1.   Using a blender or stick blender, combine
     both ingredients to make a puree.
2.   Put in a jar or tub with lid on.
3.   Keep in fridge. Preferably use
     within 3 weeks.

GREEN CHILLI PUREE

Ingredients

250g   Fresh green chillies, seeds out and
       cap removed (10-12 chillies)
4   Dst sp vegetable oil (quantity of oil can
       be increased/reduced as required)

Method

1.   Using a blender or stick blender,
     combine both ingredients, adding a little bit
     of water, to make a puree.
2.   Put in a jar or tub with lid on.
3.   Keep in fridge. Preferably use
     within 1 week.

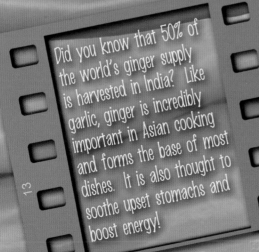

Did you know that 50% of the world's ginger supply is harvested in India? Like garlic, ginger is incredibly important in Asian cooking and forms the base of most dishes. It is also thought to soothe upset stomachs and boost energy!

Rajasthani gosht is a traditionally hot and spicy lamb dish that is best served with steamed rice or chappatis. If you can't find fresh curry leaves, soak dried ones in water, using about 20% more than fresh.

Did you know that fresh red chillies are thought to be 3 times spicier than green chillies and that dried chillies are up to 10 times hotter than fresh? Also, as a general rule, the smaller the chilli, the spicier!

Although black and green cardamoms are often substituted for each other, in Asia, the black variety is regarded as superior for spicy and rustic dishes. They are a wonderful addition to a dish because they enhance the flavours of the other ingredients.

Aslam sharing his love of cooking

RAJASTHANI GOSHT

Ingredients

1kg	Boneless lamb, cut into cubes
3	Dst sp vegetable oil
1	Medium onion, chopped
2	Dst sp garlic puree (see recipe)
1	Dst sp ginger puree (see recipe)
4	Medium tomatoes
1	Black cardamom, whole
4	Green cardamoms, crushed
6	Cloves, whole
1	Dst sp coriander seeds, ground
½	Dst sp cumin seeds, ground
1	Dst sp red chilli powder
½	Dst sp turmeric powder
6	Fresh red chillies, whole
6	Bay leaves
1	Handful of fresh coriander, chopped
8	Fresh curry leaves
½	Medium red pepper, sliced
3	Eggs, boiled and cut into small pieces (optional)
3	Dst sp natural yoghurt
1	Dst sp salt

Method

1. Put lamb, onion, garlic, ginger, tomatoes, black and green cardamoms, cloves, bay leaves, yoghurt and salt in a pan with oil and cook on a low heat for about 45 minutes or until meat is tender. Increase heat towards the end to reduce excess liquid.

2. Add ground coriander, ground cumin, red chilli powder, turmeric powder and red chillies and cook until oil separates from spices.

3. Add fresh coriander, fresh curry leaves and red pepper. Stir and leave to simmer for 5 minutes with lid on.

4. Finally, throw in boiled egg pieces (if using), stir gently and serve.

Forgiveness

During the writing of this book there has been time to reflect on qualities as being ingredients in the Aagrah recipe for success.

One that I identified and talked about earlier was the sacrifice that my family made in order to support me through many years of absence from them, both physically and emotionally. When we were preparing that text, one of my colleagues asked me "Have they forgiven you?" And I was able to say that my wife was really gifted in that regard, and that she had been able to do so.

That question made me think about how forgiveness plays out in life, as a sort of currency. We hope for it from others, but we probably also have to offer it at the same time.

The issue of forgiveness then naturally arose in my mind in reference to the arson attack on our Pudsey site. At first, everyone external to Aagrah insisted that it must be a racist attack. Within the organisation we were not happy with that conclusion. It is true that when you are attacked because of where you come from, or your gender, or the colour of your skin, these are permanent facts about you. With the best will in the world, with all the fear in the world, they are immutable. There is no promise of reprieve. It is a hopeless situation. Both as a non-white person and during the development of Aagrah, there have been attacks and negative judgements entirely because of our ethnicity. If to err is human and to forgive is divine, then I don't think I could honestly claim that I forgive these acts in that sense.

But in the case of the arson attack, for example, not only did it give us strength, as we met such great people who turned the situation round in record time so that we re-opened within five days, but it wasn't racially motivated at all. It was a business competitor.

When I think of people who have tried to make me feel small, I remind myself how fortunate I have been to know so many great people who have worked with Aagrah to make us not only commercially successful, but also socially successful and a valued contributor to our community.

When I think of my nephew Sajid and how robbed we felt when we lost him, it would be so easy not to forgive God for taking him from us. Instead, I think how knowing him brought us so many gifts, the greatest being not the success of the restaurants, but our resulting sense of family unity.

Perhaps forgiveness may be no more than just finding a place in life where something that was painful makes sense. It may mean not letting the future get chewed up by the past. It may mean letting the bad things and the bad feelings stay where they belong, with that bad event or that bad act, so that the here and now is not infected by them.

درگزر

Mr and Mrs Sabir

BANGAN ALOO

Bangan aloo is a typical Punjabi side dish, but can also be served as a main meal. It is a highly flavourful and dry dish, traditionally served with nan bread or chappatis.

Dry roasting of fenugreek seeds can reduce their supposed bitterness as well as release aromatic oils. Although largely unknown in the West, fenugreek seeds are widely used in Asian cuisine, most notably in pickles.

The aubergine took a while to become established in everyday cooking because, along with the tomato and the potato, it belongs to the deadly nightshade family and was thought to induce insanity!

Ingredients

2	Medium aubergines, very thinly sliced
500g	New potatoes, sliced
7-8	Dst sp vegetable oil
1	Medium onion, sliced
5	Cloves of garlic, crushed (or grated)
1	Medium piece of ginger, peeled and crushed (or grated)
2	Tomatoes, chopped
3-4	Green cardamoms, crushed
1	Small cinnamon stick, whole
¼	Dst sp coriander seeds, ground
¼	Dst sp cumin seeds, ground
¼	Dst sp fennel seeds, roasted
¼	Dst sp fenugreek seeds, roasted
¼	Dst sp mustard seeds
¼	Dst sp onion seeds
½	Dst sp red chilli powder
¼	Dst sp turmeric powder
3	Fresh green chillies, sliced
1	Handful of fresh coriander, chopped
1	Dst sp dried fenugreek leaves
1	Handful of fresh garden mint, chopped
1	Fresh lime, sliced
1	Red pepper, sliced
½	Dst sp sugar
½	Dst sp salt

Method

1. Heat approximately 4-5 dessertspoons of vegetable oil and shallow fry the aubergines. Leave to one side.

2. Heat remaining oil in a pan. Add onion and fry until light brown. Then add garlic and ginger and fry for at least 5 minutes.

3. Add potatoes, green cardamoms, cinnamon stick, ground coriander, ground cumin, roasted fennel and fenugreek seeds, mustard seeds and onion seeds and fry.

4. Mix in red chilli powder, turmeric powder and salt. Keep stirring on a medium heat until potatoes are nearly cooked.

5. Add sautéed aubergines, tomatoes, green chillies, fresh coriander, dried fenugreek leaves, fresh mint, lime, red pepper and sugar. Cook for a few minutes and serve.

Receiving the Choice and Heartbeat award, 1987

78

Dall achar is a satisfying and savoury pickled lentil dish. Tamarind chutney is a tangy and hot chutney that can be used as a dip, marinade or dressing and served with virtually anything.

Tamarind is a souring agent, also known as the Indian date. It is rarely used in the West, apart from, bizarrely, in the famous and popular Worcestershire sauce, which is in fact of Indian origin!

Dall or lentils are the comfort food of Asia. This essential legume contains protein, is low in fat and full of fibre. Lentils are also delicious to eat because they absorb the flavour of the spices and herbs they are cooked with.

TAMARIND CHUTNEY

Ingredients

1	Dst sp tamarind concentrate
½	Dst sp cumin seeds, crushed and roasted
1	Pinch of red chilli powder
¼	Pint water
3-4	Dst sp tomato ketchup
1	Dst sp sugar
1	Dst sp salt

Method

1. Combine all the ingredients using a blender or stick blender, until the desired consistency is achieved.
2. Keep refrigerated and eat within a week.

DALL ACHAR

Ingredients

500g	Red lentils, washed and soaked in warm water for half an hour
4	Dst sp vegetable oil
1-1½	Dst sp garlic puree (see recipe)
1	Medium tomato, cut into small pieces
½	Dst sp coriander seeds, ground
½	Dst sp cumin seeds, ground
¼	Dst sp turmeric powder
3	Fresh green chillies, chopped
1	Handful of fresh coriander, chopped
½	Dst sp mixed pickle
½	Dst sp salt

Method

1. Boil ½ litre of water, then add soaked and drained lentils with turmeric powder and salt. Cook for 7-8 minutes until lentils are soft. Add more water if required.
2. In a separate pan heat oil. Add garlic and fry on a low heat until light brown.
3. Add tomato and mixed pickle and fry for 30 seconds. Add ground coriander, ground cumin and green chillies and fry for 2 minutes. Add fresh coriander.
4. Add this mixture to the lentils. Stir and leave with lid on for a few minutes before serving.

Sabir being congratulated on winning Aagrah's first award at the original Shipley restaurant

This authentic Sindhi-style korma is far and away the most popular dish in the Aagrah restaurants due to its exceptional flavour and extensive use of spices.

This recipe was among those that won Aagrah director, Mohammed Aslam, the International Chef of the Year competition in Edinburgh, 1996. It has also won 1st prize in 'The Caterer' magazine.

Black cumin is expensive and extremely difficult to find in the UK. It is darker and sweeter than normal cumin and worth finding, but if you can't, simply substitute with the normal variety (also known as white cumin).

MURGH HYDERABADI

Ingredients

1kg	Boneless chicken, cut into cubes
5	Dst sp vegetable oil
2	Medium onions, chopped
4	Dst sp garlic puree (see recipe)
2	Dst sp ginger puree (see recipe)
5	Medium tomatoes, cut into quarters
1	Dst sp red chilli powder
¾	Dst sp turmeric powder
4	Fresh green chillies, chopped
5	Leaves of fresh coriander, cut into strips
5	Dst sp double cream
6	Dst sp natural yoghurt
1	Dst sp kewra (pandanus) water
1	Dst sp salt

The following ingredients ground together:

2	Black cardamoms (seeds only)
1	Medium cinnamon stick
5	Cloves, whole
1	Dst sp coriander seeds
½	Dst sp cumin seeds
½	Dst sp black cumin seeds
6	Black peppercorns
1	Dst sp poppy seeds
3	Bay leaves
½	Dst sp dried fenugreek leaves

Method

1. Heat oil in a pan, half fry onions and add a little water.
2. Add garlic, ginger, tomatoes, double cream and yoghurt and cook for 10 minutes on a medium heat.
3. Add the ground spices and cook for a further 5 minutes on a low heat. To avoid burning of spices add a little water.
4. Add red chilli powder, turmeric powder and salt and cook for 15 minutes. The oil should then separate and come to the top.
5. Add chicken and stir frequently until cooked through.
6. Add green chillies, fresh coriander and kewra water and cook for a few more minutes.

Hope

People often say that businesses have to grow in order to survive.

Aagrah has grown hugely, yet I think our next task will be consolidating what we have and thinking afresh about growth. In a world where the economic model of growth and expansion is now rightly being questioned, issues of sustainability are probably the biggest challenges ahead.

Perhaps it isn't so much that businesses need to grow to survive, but rather that they need to be open to change to survive.

Change is an issue of hope. When we change things or change ourselves, we do so out of a hope that this will make something or someone better. I am always hoping that we as a group will achieve this or that, that my family will attain this or that, and that I, as a person, will find out more about this or that.

I think hope is an essential part of people with vision. Not only is going forward the only direction to go in, but hope also sets targets. It is a real enemy of boredom, where people might just stand still and then backslide. Then they get lost. The duty of leadership is to give people hope, to set out things to achieve, and that keeps people united.

The entire forward motion of Aagrah, and of me as an individual, is predicated on hope. Hope is the engine that drives me. Hope is the notion that makes me think of the Hadith "If you think tomorrow is judgement day, go plant a fruit tree".

I see hope as the one thing in the world at large that can unite us all to strive for a world where we can all live. I don't mean in some sort of idyllic and benign peace. Family life has taught me that this is both unrealistic and not particularly desirable. It would be bland, and there would be no opportunities to learn new things. I am talking about a world where we challenge one another to think again about who we are, what we believe and what we do.

Hope, it seems to me, is all about uncertainty. And I think hope needs all the qualities I have discussed. It is about having a healthy sense of **fear** and a good intuition such that you choose your moment well. Hope requires that you have the **strength** to take off and **faith** that you will land, and land well. Hope means taking **responsibility** for the mistakes and any **losses** on the way, **communicating** them as best you can to those who are affected, retaining good **humour** and hoping against hope that you will be **forgiven**.

I think we probably get the capacity to hope from the **past**.

امید

Three brothers...

Machli kebabs are crisp, sharp and fragrant tuna patties. The chauri masala drumsticks are incredibly crispy and light. Both dishes can be served as starters or as part of the main meal.

84

MACHLI KEBAB

Ingredients

- 2 185g tins of tuna chunks in spring water
- 2 Dst sp vegetable oil (for frying)
- 2 Dst sp onion, very finely chopped
- 1 Dst sp crushed red chilli
- 1 Dst sp coriander seeds, crushed
- ½ Dst sp cumin seeds, ground
- 1 Dst sp lemon juice
- 1 Egg
- 2 Dst sp gram flour
- ½ Dst sp salt

Method

1. Drain water out of tuna. Mix together all the ingredients except tuna and oil. Add tuna and mix thoroughly.
2. Make kebab or burger shapes in the size of your choice.
3. Heat oil in non-stick frying pan. Shallow fry both sides of the kebabs and serve with green mint chutney (see recipe) or a chutney of your choice.

CHAURI MASALA

Ingredients

- 1kg Drumsticks (skin on or off), washed and dried
- 2 Dst sp mustard oil
- 1 Dst sp crushed red chilli
- 2 Dst sp coriander seeds, crushed
- 1 Dst sp cumin seeds, ground
- 1 Fresh lime, juiced
- 2 Dst sp salt

Method

1. Put drumsticks in a bowl and add oil, lime juice and salt.
2. Sprinkle rest of ingredients on top and mix together.
3. Place drumsticks on an oiled tray, cover with tin foil and cook in the oven at 200°C for 45 minutes.
4. Serve with green mint chutney (see recipe) or a chutney of your choice.

Chauri masala is definitely a domestic Kashmiri recipe! It isn't served in restaurants because the drumsticks do not keep and have to be eaten immediately. Machli kebabs are great because you can have them cold in sandwiches the next day!

Did you know that there are four main types of peppercorn? Black is the strongest and most common. White is sometimes used to avoid black specks. Green peppercorns are mild and soft, usually pickled and then eaten whole, and pink are in fact dried berries with a mild, peppery flavour.

Two ruffians strike again...!

Aloo methi is a dry dish with a sweet and aromatic flavour. As a final touch, lightly roast some dried methi (fenugreek) leaves in a dry pan. Then crush between your palms and sprinkle over the finished dish.

13

13

86

ALOO METHI

Ingredients

1kg	New potatoes, cut into small pieces
6	Dst sp vegetable oil
½	Small onion, sliced
2	Dst sp garlic puree (see recipe)
1	Medium tomato, chopped
1	Dst sp coriander seeds, ground
1	Dst sp cumin seeds, ground
½	Dst sp asafoetida powder
¼	Dst sp garam masala
¼	Dst sp red chilli powder
¼	Dst sp turmeric powder
4-5	Fresh red chillies, whole
1	Handful of fresh coriander, chopped
1	Dst sp dried fenugreek leaves
1	Bunch of fresh fenugreek (whole leaves only)
2	Dst sp natural yoghurt
½	Dst sp salt

Method

1. Heat oil and fry onions until light brown.
2. Add garlic and asafoetida powder and fry for 3 minutes.
3. Add tomato, red chilli powder, turmeric powder, red chillies, yoghurt and salt and cook for 2-3 minutes.
4. Add potatoes, ground coriander, ground cumin and fresh fenugreek leaves. Mix together, cover with lid and cook on a very low heat for 15-20 minutes or until potatoes are cooked through.
5. Increase the heat and keep stirring to avoid sticking. Add garam masala, fresh coriander and dried fenugreek leaves and mix thoroughly. Cover again with lid and serve after 10 minutes.

Although they are called seeds, coriander seeds are in fact the fruit of the coriander plant. Interestingly, the pleasing aromatic oil from these 'seeds' is often used in the manufacture of beauty products.

Methi or fenugreek leaves are high in iron and are believed to have medicinal properties. Use the leaves whole and do not add the stalks. If you can't find fresh methi, you can use dried methi for the taste and spinach as a substitute for texture.

Nihari gosht is an extremely tender lamb dish with a thick sauce. To make it gluten-free use cornflour instead of wheat flour. The flavour will be slightly different, but the thickening effect will be the same.

Nihari gosht translates as 'breakfast lamb'. In Asia, this meal is left to cook all night on a low heat (probably originally to ensure that tough meat was tenderised). This smooth and mild dish is then traditionally eaten for breakfast with nan bread.

88

Sabir

NIHARI GOSHT

Ingredients

1kg	Boneless lamb, diced (5cm cubes)
6	Dst sp vegetable oil
1	Medium onion, chopped
1	Dst sp garlic puree (see recipe)
1	Dst sp ginger puree (see recipe)
1	Small piece of ginger, cut into small sticks (for garnish)
2	Medium tomatoes, chopped
1	Dst sp coriander seeds, ground
½	Dst sp cumin seeds, ground
¼	Dst sp fennel seeds
½	Dst sp red chilli powder
½	Dst sp turmeric powder
2	Fresh green chillies, sliced
2	Fresh green chillies, finely chopped (for garnish)
1	Pinch of fresh coriander (for garnish)
½	Dst sp dried fenugreek leaves
1-1½	Dst sp wheat flour, soaked in water to make thin batter
½	Dst sp salt

The following ingredients ground together:

4	Green cardamoms, whole
1	Medium cinnamon stick
1	Star anise (whole star including shell)
4	Bay leaves

Method

1. Heat oil in pan and fry onion until light brown.
2. Add garlic and ginger and fry for a few minutes.
3. Add lamb, tomatoes and sliced green chillies and cook for a few more minutes until lamb is sealed.
4. Add red chilli powder, turmeric powder and salt and cook for 3 minutes.
5. Add ground coriander, ground cumin, fennel seeds, dried fenugreek leaves and the mixed ground spices. Cook for a few minutes and then add wheat flour batter. Add a little water and cook for 2 minutes.
6. Add ¼ litre of water and bring to the boil. Cover with lid and cook on a low heat for about half an hour until lamb is tender and sauce has thickened. Add more water or wheat flour batter as required.
7. Garnish with small sticks of ginger, finely chopped green chilli and a pinch of fresh coriander before serving.

Star anise is one of the most beautiful spices in the world. Native to South China, the star seed is a warm, sweet and aromatic spice. In Asia it is used mostly in meat dishes and adds a liquorice flavour.

Saltaire Road Shipley

4 Saltaire Road, Shipley, BD18 3HN

T: 01274 530 880

Westgate Shipley

27 Westgate, Shipley, BD18 3QX

T: 01274 583 338

Pudsey

483 Bradford Road, Pudsey, LS28 8ED

T: 01274 668 818

Skipton

Devonshire Place, Keighley Road,

Skipton, BD23 2LR

T: 01756 790 807

Garforth

Aberford Road, Garforth, LS25 2HF

T: 0113 287 0606

Doncaster

Great North Road, Woodlands, Doncaster, DN6 7RA

T: **01302 728 888**

Tadcaster

York Road, Steeton, Tadcaster, Nr York, LS24 8EG

T: **01937 530 888**

Wakefield

Barnsley Road, Sandal, Wakefield, WF1 5NX

T: **01924 242 222**

Denby Dale

250 Wakefield Road, Denby Dale,

Huddersfield, HD8 8SU

T: **01484 866 266**

Leeds City

St Peter's Square, Quarry Hill, Leeds, LS9 8AH

T: **0113 245 5667**

EDITOR'S CHEAT NOTES

I made every recipe in this book (there are 39) in my little flat in Birmingham city centre in the space of about 3 weeks. I went from curry appreciator to curry lover, expert and connoisseur. Having said that, I don't think my boyfriend or I will ever look at curry in the same light again. And all this was before I had even met Aslam or any of the Aagrah crew.

The learning curve was steep and it is for that reason that I persuaded the publisher to give me my own page; I decided very early on that I wanted to make my (incredibly intense) experience count for something. So I have put together a collection of what I call 'cheat notes' to try and ensure that the learning curve is less daunting for you guys using this book, and so that you can get on with your curry cooking as soon as possible.

Beginner's shopping list
The beauty of Asian cooking is that if you equip your kitchen with the basics you can cook almost any curry. All you have to do then is buy the main ingredient, be it chicken or lentils, and any more unusual herbs and spices. Your newfound Asian cookery pantry should contain the following staples (first two columns):

Essentials	Fresh ingredients	For the more adventurous recipes!...
Vegetable/olive oil/ghee	(best bought on day of use)	Ajwain (carom) seeds
Basmati rice	Onions	Crushed red chilli
Cardamoms (green and black)	Garlic	Fennel seeds
Cinnamon sticks	Ginger	Fenugreek seeds
Cloves	Tomatoes	Mustard seeds
Coriander seeds	Chillies	Onion seeds
Cumin seeds	Fresh coriander leaves	Pomegranate seeds
Black peppercorns	Fresh curry leaves	Star anise
Red chilli powder	Fresh fenugreek leaves	Amchoor (mango powder)
Turmeric powder	Fresh mint leaves	Asafoetida powder
Dried bay leaves	Limes	Kewra (pandanus) water
Dried curry leaves	Other vegetables, as needed	Rose water
Dried fenugreek leaves	Cream	Saffron
Salt	Yoghurt	

Getting started
Before you begin cooking, I recommend that you grind cumin and coriander seeds and make garlic and ginger purees (see recipes) as these essential ingredients are used in most Asian dishes.

Crushed versus ground

Crushed spices are spices that have been cracked using a pestle and mortar, or simply crushed between a board and the back of a spoon. To grind spices, use a coffee grinder (although you may not want to use this for coffee afterwards!), electric food processor/blender or electric pepper and spice grinder/mill.

What is a dessertspoon anyway?

The dessertspoon (abbreviated in this book as dst sp) is a medium-sized spoon, intermediate in size between a tablespoon and a teaspoon.

Finding ingredients

The following ingredients may be hard to find: mustard oil, ajwain (carom) seeds, pomegranate seeds, fresh bay, curry and fenugreek leaves and kewra (pandanus) water. Try your local Asian shop or market, or, failing that, the Internet!

Special diets and substitutions

Aslam was always very clear about the Asian method of cooking; always feel free to vary the ingredients to suit your taste/requirements. If you don't like overly spicy food, add less spices. If you're vegan, use oil instead of butter.

Suggested substitutions:

If you can't find:	Use:
Monkfish	Coley, lobster meat, scallops
Mustard oil	Vegetable oil
Black cumin seeds	Normal (white) cumin seeds
Pomegranate seeds (dried)	Pomegranate (anardana) powder
Fresh bay leaves	Dried bay leaves
Fresh curry/fenugreek leaves	Dried leaves; soak and use about 20% more
Green sultanas	Normal sultanas
Kewra (pandanus) water	Rose water
Chappati flour	Whole wheat flour
Balti dish	Wok

Chilli advice

Always use the recommended quantity of turmeric as this counteracts chilli. To make chillies less spicy, chop out the seeds and the flesh that holds the seeds in place.

Finally, I need to thank Colin Elsworth, Frances Baines, Katie and Peter Trethewey, Catherine Wyatt and Tom Parker for their eating assistance in what I now call Curry Month, January 2005!

Florence Millett
Editor

93

EPILOGUE

Bradford, it could be argued, holds a unique place in modern Britain as an example of the multitude of ways in which a multicultural society can define itself and succeed. This process of self-definition, followed by success, has been demonstrated in government, in education, in public service delivery, and, above all, in the community.

In the 1960s, Bradford was primarily a textile-producing town, characterised by the 'dark satanic mills' long associated with the West Riding of Yorkshire. Already in steady economic decline, the industry, and Bradford generally, took more and more of its labour force from a stream of new immigrants. These people came to Bradford to escape grim rural poverty in their own countries, often only to descend deeply into the UK's own equally brutal urban version.

A series of events highlighting the negative turbulence of these times came to national attention following the riots of 1976, and was positively balanced, just as dramatically, in 1985 by the election of Mohammed Ajeeb as the UK's first Asian mayor.

For some, Bradford became a pariah, a vision of a terrible future for a nation divided by religion, race and culture.

As it turns out, these people were wrong.

I write this last sentence as though somehow this was an easy transformation, or one that just happened by chance. As an immigrant to the UK myself, with a childhood and youth shaped by the struggle in my native land for labour and civil rights, I know from experience that nothing could be further from the truth. In order to resolve their differences at local level and to promote this city as among the most culturally vibrant in the country, the people of Bradford must have worked tirelessly and imaginatively.

The Aagrah family have been at the forefront of both of these activities. They have continuously supported the efforts of the City of Bradford to show how the best can be achieved there using many of the component parts of a multicultural city. Their chain of authentic Asian restaurants is second to none, as their many awards testify. Their record as an employer is enviable. As ambassadors for their city, they are indefatigable supporters of all that is good about coming to and coming from Bradford.

Bradford's tasks ahead will always be a challenge. The endeavour to manage well the needs, hopes, dreams and wishes of so diverse a population provides perennial opportunities to be creative. Aslam's recognition of the qualities needed for success is a reminder of the universal nature of humankind, and how, as Bradfordians, the Aagrah family stands as a positive symbol of what multiculturalism can mean.

When we first met with Aslam, it was of course to discuss the creation of a cookbook, whereby the Aagrah recipes could be passed over to their customers and enable them to make the food at home. Aslam was adamant that his recipes should be seen as a guide; that practice makes perfect, and by perfect he meant perfect for each individual's taste.

The fact that this book was conceived to pass on recipes to others makes it, by any standards, a conventional cookbook. It contains the lists of ingredients and techniques needed to create the dishes that have ensured Aagrah's inclusion in such diverse publications as the Michelin Guide, the Real Restaurant Guide and Pat Chapman's Cobra Good Curry Guide. In this way, **Hand over Fist** is a predictable cookbook; buy this, chop that, cook it in this way, aim for that result. And there is nothing wrong with that.

But in terms of Aagrah as a company and what has been achieved, we felt there was another recipe at work that could account for the remarkable loyalty of their many customers, some of whom have been eating regularly with Aagrah for more than 25 years. We thought it might explain how more than 12 members of Aslam's family continue to work in the business day in day out, some even having returned to work in catering, although many have professional qualifications. It may also explain why, in turn, many other members of his family support them from home. And we also felt that it keyed into the relationship between Aagrah and the Bradford area as a whole. Perhaps this other recipe accounts for the terrific staff at Aagrah who give attention to both detail and service, without which the Aagrah chain would not enjoy the success it does.

So we asked Aslam to try and name the 10 most important qualities needed to develop Aagrah. By identifying these qualities, we think he has also given us some sort of universal guide to success which can be applied to any venture. These qualities have provided the cookbook with a second structure that is not so conventional.

It is no accident that this fourth in the HAND series is called **Hand over Fist**. 'Hand over fist' is a turn of phrase usually used to define success, and Aagrah certainly have that. But in the context of the Aagrah cookbook, it also stands for the way in which Aslam's family has demonstrated how, as immigrants and as Muslims, the best of their culture has combined with the best of British culture. Hands have won out over fists and all have benefited as a result.

The previous books in the HAND series have all concentrated on how this recipe or that approach will improve your body's physical health. At ENDpapers we believe that **Hand over Fist** extends this focus on personal health with authentic recipes from Kashmir and a philosophy that can improve our communities' social health.

Magdalena Chávez
Originator of the HAND series

95

CREDITS

Many people have worked to make this book a reality.

First, without the Aagrah family there would have been nothing to make a book about; Mr Mohammed Sabir, Mr Zafar Iqbal, Mr Arshad Mahmood, Mr Naeem Aslam, Mr Tariq Mahmood, Mr Wasim Aslam, Mr Tahir Iqbal and the entire Aagrah team.

Behind all of these people are the families who put up with the long hours of work and absence from home. Everyone at Aagrah acknowledges their enduring and devoted support.

The profile that we enjoy has been built painstakingly over many years. Simon Dunn and Richard Knill have each done a great job in helping communicate the aims and objectives of all our activities. I thank them both.

Peter Nightingale, thank you for being my motivation.

As Bradfordians, we are immensely proud of our city. It has been a pleasure indeed to have been honoured by the spirit of the people, especially in Shipley, which is the home of Aagrah.

Having fellow Yorkshireman and distinguished chef Brian Turner contribute the foreword of this book has further underlined our pride in the North and in Britain as a whole.

The making of a book takes many skills and talents. The team at ENDpapers included Catherine Lucas who has worked painstakingly to create the book's rich look and Florence Millett who tried all of the recipes in her domestic and non-Asian kitchen and then worked with me on the anecdotes throughout the text. Safina Sabir, Trang La, Iqbal Shah, Julia Key and Sally Mowbray were in constant communication to source the photos and ensure the contents were right, and in the right place. Magdalena Chávez and I spent long hours in conversation, through which the qualities were identified and developed.

Hand over Fist may have my name on the front, but, in reality, it represents many people's efforts and I am proud to have worked with each one of them.

Mohammed Aslam
The Aagrah Group
August 2005

- Easy to use

- Excellent for those with dietary restrictions

- Based on the flavourful vegan, gluten free and vegetarian restaurant El Piano, York

1st in the HAND series

- Beautifully illustrated throughout

- Anecdotes throughout

HAND TO MOUTH

NO ORDINARY COOKBOOK

foreword by Hugh Bayley MP

Magdalena Chávez
Lisa Sharman
Rachel Stainsby

- Ideal for children and beginner cooks

- Vegetarian throughout

- Key-coded recipes to guide ability

- Written with children for children

2nd in the HAND series

- Bright and colourful

- Stories, puzzles and tips

HAND in HAND

An extraordinary COOKBOOK!!!

Sally Mowbray
Rosey Hill
Katie Ireland

MOWBRAY • HILL • IRELAND

- Traditional favourites with all the flavour left in, but none of the fat

- Low sodium throughout

- Nutritional and medical information and tables on each page

3rd in the HAND series

- All from Emmy® award - winning doctor and chef Tim Harlan, as seen on the UKTV Food channel

a perfectly ordinary cookbook

Hand on Heart

Dr Tim Harlan